A Satellite Account to Measure the Retail Transformation

Organizational, Conceptual, and Data Foundations

Panel on Measuring the Transformation of
Retail Trade and Related Activities

Committee on National Statistics

Division of Behavioral and Social Sciences and Education

A Consensus Study Report of

The National Academies of
SCIENCES · ENGINEERING · MEDICINE

THE NATIONAL ACADEMIES PRESS
Washington, DC
www.nap.edu

THE NATIONAL ACADEMIES PRESS   500 Fifth Street, NW   Washington, DC 20001

This activity was supported by a contract between the National Academy of Sciences and the U.S. Department of Labor, Bureau of Labor Statistics, under Contract No. 1625 DC-19-C-0009. Support for the work of the Committee on National Statistics is provided by a consortium of federal agencies through a grant from the National Science Foundation, a National Agricultural Statistics Service cooperative agreement, and several individual contracts. Any opinions, findings, conclusions, or recommendations expressed in this publication do not necessarily reflect the views of any organization or agency that provided support for the project.

International Standard Book Number-13: 978-0-309-38153-6
International Standard Book Number-10: 0-309-38153-3
Digital Object Identifier: https://doi.org/10.17226/26101

Additional copies of this publication are available from the National Academies Press, 500 Fifth Street, NW, Keck 360, Washington, DC 20001; (800) 624-6242 or (202) 334-3313; http://www.nap.edu.

Copyright 2021 by the National Academy of Sciences. All rights reserved.

Printed in the United States of America

Suggested citation: National Academies of Sciences, Engineering, and Medicine. (2021). *A Satellite Account to Measure the Retail Transformation: Organizational, Conceptual, and Data Foundations*. Washington, DC: The National Academies Press. https://doi.org/10.17226/26101.

The National Academies of
SCIENCES · ENGINEERING · MEDICINE

The **National Academy of Sciences** was established in 1863 by an Act of Congress, signed by President Lincoln, as a private, nongovernmental institution to advise the nation on issues related to science and technology. Members are elected by their peers for outstanding contributions to research. Dr. Marcia McNutt is president.

The **National Academy of Engineering** was established in 1964 under the charter of the National Academy of Sciences to bring the practices of engineering to advising the nation. Members are elected by their peers for extraordinary contributions to engineering. Dr. John L. Anderson is president.

The **National Academy of Medicine** (formerly the Institute of Medicine) was established in 1970 under the charter of the National Academy of Sciences to advise the nation on medical and health issues. Members are elected by their peers for distinguished contributions to medicine and health. Dr. Victor J. Dzau is president.

The three Academies work together as the **National Academies of Sciences, Engineering, and Medicine** to provide independent, objective analysis and advice to the nation and conduct other activities to solve complex problems and inform public policy decisions. The National Academies also encourage education and research, recognize outstanding contributions to knowledge, and increase public understanding in matters of science, engineering, and medicine.

Learn more about the National Academies of Sciences, Engineering, and Medicine at **www.nationalacademies.org**.

The National Academies of
SCIENCES • ENGINEERING • MEDICINE

Consensus Study Reports published by the National Academies of Sciences, Engineering, and Medicine document the evidence-based consensus on the study's statement of task by an authoring committee of experts. Reports typically include findings, conclusions, and recommendations based on information gathered by the committee and the committee's deliberations. Each report has been subjected to a rigorous and independent peer-review process and it represents the position of the National Academies on the statement of task.

Proceedings published by the National Academies of Sciences, Engineering, and Medicine chronicle the presentations and discussions at a workshop, symposium, or other event convened by the National Academies. The statements and opinions contained in proceedings are those of the participants and are not endorsed by other participants, the planning committee, or the National Academies.

For information about other products and activities of the National Academies, please visit www.nationalacademies.org/about/whatwedo.

PANEL ON MEASURING THE TRANSFORMATION OF RETAIL TRADE AND RELATED ACTIVITIES

J. STEVEN LANDEFELD (*Chair*), Consultant and former director, Bureau of Economic Analysis, Washington, DC
CAROL A. CORRADO, The Conference Board, Washington, DC
GREGORY DUNCAN, Amazon and University of Washington
TERESA C. FORT, Dartmouth College
JOHN C. HALTIWANGER, University of Maryland, College Park
DALE W. JORGENSON, Harvard University
MICHAEL MANDEL, Progressive Policy Institute, Washington, DC
KELLY MCCONVILLE, Reed College
LEONARD I. NAKAMURA, Federal Reserve Bank of Philadelphia
WESLEY YUNG, Statistics Canada, Ottawa, Ontario

STUART ELLIOTT, *Co-study Director*
NANCY KIRKENDALL, *Co-study Director*
ANTHONY MANN, *Program Associate*
ELLIS GRIMES, *Senior Program Assistant*

COMMITTEE ON NATIONAL STATISTICS

ROBERT M. GROVES (*Chair*), Office of the Provost, Georgetown University
LAWRENCE D. BOBO, Department of Sociology, Harvard University
ANNE C. CASE, Woodrow Wilson School of Public and International Affairs, Princeton University
MICK P. COUPER, Institute for Social Research, University of Michigan
JANET M. CURRIE, Woodrow Wilson School of Public and International Affairs, Princeton University
DIANA FARRELL, JPMorgan Chase Institute, Washington, DC
ROBERT GOERGE, Chapin Hall at the University of Chicago
ERICA L. GROSHEN, School of Industrial and Labor Relations, Cornell University
HILARY HOYNES, Goldman School of Public Policy, University of California, Berkeley
DANIEL KIFER, Department of Computer Science and Engineering, The Pennsylvania State University
SHARON LOHR, School of Mathematical and Statistical Sciences, Arizona State University, *Emerita*
JEROME P. REITER, Department of Statistical Science, Duke University
JUDITH A. SELTZER, Department of Sociology, University of California, Los Angeles
C. MATTHEW SNIPP, School of the Humanities and Sciences, Stanford University
ELIZABETH A. STUART, Department of Mental Health, Johns Hopkins Bloomberg School of Public Health
JEANNETTE WING, Data Science Institute and Computer Science Department, Columbia University

BRIAN HARRIS-KOJETIN, *Director*
CONSTANCE F. CITRO, *Senior Scholar*

Acknowledgments

This report reflects the contributions of many colleagues who generously gave their time and expert advice in helping prepare the panel's report on measuring the transformation of retail trade and its activities.

The panel thanks Bureau of Labor Statistics (BLS) Commissioner William Beach and Associate Commissioner Lucy Eldridge for their help in understanding the challenges confronting measurement of retail trade and in shaping the scope of the study. We also thank BLS staff, in particular the panel's main contacts at BLS—Jenny Rudd, Chris Sparks, and Chris Manning—who worked within BLS to find answers to questions the panel raised throughout the study; Chet Myers, Jenny Rudd, Kandi Miller, and Brian Chansky for their background briefings at the first panel meeting; and Ken Robertson, Matthew Russell, Brian Chansky, Brendan Williams, Bonnie Murphy, and Dominic Smith for their presentations and discussions at the panel's workshop, which helped us to understand key conceptual, methodological, and source-data issues.

The panel also benefited greatly from presentations on topics central to the panel's charge in measuring the transformation of retail trade, made by experts from the Bureau of Economic Analysis (BEA) (Jon D. Samuels, Tina Highfill, and Ana Aizcorbe) and the Census Bureau (Emek Basker, Ian Thomas, and Edward Watkins). A number of other experts at BEA and Census also helped in providing important insights in understanding current and alternative estimates of retail trade; in particular, I was greatly helped by Erich Strassner, Edward Morgan, and Thomas Howells at BEA.

We are also grateful for the presentations by, and discussions with, experts from academia, business, international organizations, and the

Federal Reserve Board. These experts provided perspective on researchers' and other data users' views of the forces transforming retail trade, the statistical challenges in measuring the change, and suggestions for addressing needed changes in measurement: Chad Syverson (University of Chicago), Steve Noble (McKinsey and Company), Jack Kleinhenz (National Retail Federation), Drew Spata (Macy's), David Glick (FLEXE), Richard Phillips (Yale Divinity School and former CEO of Pilot Freight Services), Anne Goodchild (University of Washington), Leland Crane (Federal Reserve Board), Phillip Smith (Statistics Canada), Marshall Reinsdorf (International Monetary Fund), and Robert Feenstra (University of California, Davis).

The panel could not have conducted its work efficiently without the capable staff of the National Academies of Sciences, Engineering, and Medicine, including Brian Harris-Kojetin, director of CNSTAT, and Constance Citro, senior scholar, who helped in framing the task for the panel, advising on specific issues during the panel study, and making important suggestions on the presentation of the panel conclusions and recommendations. Nancy Kirkendall and Stuart Elliott did an outstanding job in working with the panel to distill and summarize a broad range of complex topics to support the conclusions and recommendations presented in the report.

Finally, and most importantly, I would like to add a note of appreciation for my fellow panel members who formed the core of the study team. Panel members helped in developing the focus, identifying and prioritizing the challenges and solutions, making presentations, chairing sessions, acting as discussants, drafting materials, providing detailed information in their areas of expertise, and reviewing and commenting on multiple rounds of workshop summaries and drafts of the report.

This Consensus Study Report was reviewed in draft form by individuals chosen for their diverse perspectives and technical expertise. The purpose of this independent review is to provide candid and critical comments that will assist the National Academies in making each published report as sound as possible and to ensure that it meets the institutional standards for quality, objectivity, evidence, and responsiveness to the study charge. The review comments and draft manuscript remain confidential to protect the integrity of the deliberative process.

We thank the following individuals for their review of this report: Emek M. Basker, Center for Economic Studies, U.S. Census Bureau; Thomas J. Holmes, Department of Economics, University of Minnesota; Thomas L. Mesenbourg, Jr., former U.S. Census Bureau; Colm A. O'Muircheartaigh, Harris School of Public Policy, NORC at the University of Chicago; Ariel Pakes, Department of Economics, Harvard University; Richard G. Phillips, Yale Divinity School, former chair and CEO of Pilot Freight Services; and Chad Syverson, Booth School of Business, University of Chicago.

Although the reviewers listed above provided many constructive comments and suggestions, they were not asked to endorse the conclusions or recommendations of this report nor did they see the final draft before its release. The review of this report was overseen by Charles F. Manski, Department of Economics, Northwestern University. He was responsible for making certain that an independent examination of this report was carried out in accordance with the standards of the National Academies and that all review comments were carefully considered. Responsibility for the final content rests entirely with the authoring committee and the National Academies.

J. Steven Landefeld, *Chair*
Panel on Measuring the Transformation
of Retail Trade and Related Activities

Contents

Summary   1

1   Introduction   9
    The Panel's Approach, 11

2   Transformation of the Retail Sector   13
    Recent Changes in the Retail Sector, 14
    How Recent Retail Changes Relate to the Basic Definition
        of the Sector, 20
    The Retail Transformation as Seen in Existing Statistical
        Series, 23

3   Measuring Retail Employment and Labor Productivity   29
    Measuring Retail Employment and Labor Productivity:
        The High-Level Task, 30
    Defining the Retail Sector, 32
    Measuring Output, 43
    Adjusting Nominal Output for Changes in Prices, 55
    Measuring Input, 62
    Additional Data Sources, 65

4   Toward a Retail Satellite Account   73
    What Are Satellite Accounts and How Are They Used?, 74
    Audiences for a Retail Related Satellite Account and Measures
        of Employment and Productivity, 76

    Defining a Retail-Supporting Sector, 78
    Existing Satellite Accounts with Potentially Useful Features, 84

5 Recommendations for a Retail Satellite Account   89
    Motivation and Overarching Recommendations, 90
    Design of a Satellite Account (Specifications), 92
    Studying and Solving Data Issues, 97

References   103

Appendixes

A Agenda for the Panel's Workshop   107
B Retail Output, Hours, and Labor Productivity, 1997-2018   111
C Biographical Sketches of Panel Members   113

Boxes, Figures, and Tables

BOXES

1-1 Statement of Task, 10

3-1 Labor Productivity for Trade-Related Industries: How It Is Measured by the Bureau of Labor Statistics, 31
3-2 Measuring the Economy: The North American Industry Classification System (NAICS), 33
3-3 NAICS Classification and Designation of Auxiliaries, 36
3-4 Alternative Measures of Nominal Output, 45
3-5 The Census Bureau's Annual Economic Surveys, 49
3-6 The Census Bureau's 5-Year Surveys, 51
3-7 BLS Data on Employment and Hours for Trade-Related Industries, 63
3-8 Census Bureau's Other Important Annual Survey, 65

4-1 System of National Accounts, 75
4-2 Evaluation Criteria, 77
4-3 Four Alternative Definitions of a Retail-Related Sector, 79

FIGURES

2-1 Average annual change in labor productivity, 1997-2018, by type of output measure, 24

4-1a Comparison of distributional and retail-supporting industry codes, 80
4-1b Comparison of retail-controlled and enterprise-based industry codes, 80

TABLES

2-1   Several Indicators of the Retail Transformation, 1997-2019 (percentage), 26

3-1a Comparison of the Number of Establishments by NAICS Codes, as Measured by Three Programs, 2017, 42
3-1b Comparison of the Estimated Number of Employees by NAICS Codes, as Measured by Three Programs, 42
3-2   Number of Auxiliary Establishments That Supported Retail Trade, 2012 Economic Census, 54

App B Retail Output, Hours, and Labor Productivity, 1997-2018, 112

Summary

The Bureau of Labor Statistics (BLS) asked the Committee on National Statistics (CNSTAT) of the National Academies of Sciences, Engineering, and Medicine to evaluate changes in the retail trade sector since the 1990s, assess measures of employment and labor productivity for the sector, and discuss the value and specifications for a satellite account to measure retail-related employment and labor productivity that would better capture the transformation. The request was motivated in part by shifts in the ways that warehouses, transportation, and delivery services are now supporting retail, which are not reflected in retail employment and labor productivity statistics.

The panel's primary information-gathering activity was to hold a workshop that provided input from researchers, industry representatives, data users, and relevant statistical agencies. The workshop supplemented the panel's expertise on the economics and statistics of the retail sector with the expertise of additional economists who have studied the retail sector, experts who understand the details of current government statistical programs, and industry representatives. The panel took a broad approach in reviewing options for a retail-related satellite account, considering both pragmatic immediate steps and aspirational longer-term goals. It also identified ways to progress toward the aspirational goals by carrying out specific analyses, collecting additional data, and conducting case studies.

TRANSFORMATION OF THE RETAIL SECTOR

The retail sector has experienced a number of important changes over the past few decades in both the way it is structured and the nature of the goods and services it provides. These changes include the rise of warehouse clubs and supercenters; the rise of e-commerce; the digital transformation of some retail goods, such as books, music, and video; the increase in imports of retail goods and services; the role of large firms in driving the transformation in retail; increased product variety and the role of retail firms in presenting and organizing products; and recent changes in response to COVID-19 that have in turn heightened some longer-term trends.

As a result of these changes, the cost structure of large retailers is now often quite different from that of small retailers (**Conclusion 2-1**). Large retailers often provide wholesale, warehousing, and transportation services directly, whereas small retailers usually purchase these services. In addition, large retailers sometimes outsource some traditional retail services, such as customer service and order fulfilment, whereas small retailers usually provide these services directly. This difference in cost structures between large and small retailers heightens the importance of using measures of employment and labor productivity that can be meaningfully compared across retailers that are structured differently.

The recent transformation in the retail sector has also shifted some retail services outside the traditional definition of the sector, for example shifting videos from sales to leasing. It has also brought some services into retail that were formerly outside the traditional definition, such as providing delivery services for e-commerce purchases (**Conclusion 2-2**). Where this has taken place, an understanding of the employment and productivity effect of the changes will require analyses that compare services inside and outside the traditional retail sector.

Beyond these specific changes, the dynamic nature of the retail sector ensures that new—and as yet unknown—changes will regularly appear in the years ahead to challenge available measures of employment and labor productivity. This dynamic nature raises an additional challenge to efforts to track the ongoing transformation in retail and continue to adapt retail-related measures over time.

MEASURING RETAIL EMPLOYMENT AND LABOR PRODUCTIVTY

The U.S. statistical programs that collect retail-related data provide a framework for measuring retail employment and labor productivity, but they also have some notable constraints. Calculating labor productivity involves estimating the real output of the retail sector and dividing it by the hours worked in the sector. All aspects of this simple definition pose conceptual and practical measurement difficulties.

Federal economic data are collected by industry according to the North American Industry Classification System (NAICS), which classifies establishments hierarchically according to their business processes. Although this system usefully groups together similar business establishments in providing data, it specifically separates wholesale, warehousing, and transportation services into their own industries, even though large retailers are now increasingly integrating these functions into their retail operations. Similarly, retail transactions that take place through leasing rather than sales or through digital products appear in entirely different industries. As a result, the way the data are currently collected makes it difficult to identify the portion of wholesale, warehousing, and transportation services, or the portion of leasing or digital transactions that are closely related to retail trade and could be usefully analyzed as part of a broader retail-related sector. A study of a broader retail sector will require estimates of the retail-related portion of industries—such as warehousing—where the relevant NAICS codes are only partially related to retail (**Conclusion 3-1**).

Labor productivity measures are calculated with data provided by two different agencies—BLS and Census—that use separate business registers with separate classifications of business establishments as sampling frames for their surveys to estimate output (Census), price deflators (BLS), and labor input (BLS). The differences between these sampling frames likely contribute to error in the labor productivity estimates (**Conclusion 3-2**). This error could be investigated and a reconciliation could be undertaken between the two business lists (**Conclusion 3-3**), and that in turn could be used to develop factors to adjust for the effects of any systematic differences between them (**Conclusion 3-4**). The ideal long-term solution would be for the federal government to develop and use a single common business register (**Conclusion 3-5**).

The nominal output of the retail sector is defined in four different ways in the federal statistical system: (1) as total sales revenue; (2) as the difference between sales revenue and the cost of goods sold (gross margin); (3) as the difference between sales revenue and the cost of all purchased inputs (value added); and (4) as the difference between sales revenue and the cost of all inputs purchased within the sector (sectoral output). For narrowly defined sectors, the sectoral output measure is effectively sales revenue, but as the scope of a sector becomes increasingly broad the sectoral output measure moves toward a value-added measure.[1]

A sales revenue measure of output is the simplest to produce, but it does not reflect changes in a retailer's cost structure when additional functions—like warehousing—are integrated into the business. A value-added measure of output is theoretically preferred for measuring labor productivity in retail, capturing the difference between gross output and intermediate

---

[1] The term "gross output" is used across sectors by the U.S. Bureau of Economic Analysis (BEA) to refer to a gross margin measure for retail and wholesale trade and a sales revenue measure for all other sectors.

inputs. However, it requires estimating all noncapital purchased inputs, not just goods purchased. Comprehensive measures of value-added at the industry level rely on input-output accounts that have limitations in source data, including the frequency of updates. A gross margin measure of output for retail and wholesale trade reflects the value of the most important input for a retailer—the cost of goods sold—while sidestepping problems related to estimating other inputs (**Conclusion 3-6**). For retail-supporting services that might be combined with retail trade in a broader retail-related sector, similar choices are necessary concerning which measure of nominal output to use, although the gross margin concept applies only to retail and wholesale trade.

The Economic Census and the Economic Surveys provide limited data on purchases and operating expenses for computing gross margin and value-added output measures, respectively. These data limitations limit the level of industry detail and frequency for gross margin and value-added measures of retail output. They also offer limited data for estimating which support establishments in a firm ("auxiliaries") support its retail establishments and to what extent (**Conclusion 3-7**). Private-sector data could potentially provide more timely information about economic output (**Conclusion 3-12**).

Nominal output must be adjusted by price changes to identify the real changes in the output of the sector. The price adjustment step is crucial, because price changes can accentuate or mask any real changes that are occurring, particularly during a period of rapid change when goods and services are evolving and are hard to compare over time. Conceptually, the key price adjustment that needs to take place for the retail sector itself relates to the *services* the sector provides, with respect to changes in the prices of those services and adjustment for changes in their quality. This differs from price adjustment related to the products the retailer sells, which focuses on the characteristics of the goods themselves. Price deflation in the retail sector needs to consider, for example, the shifts in services in moving from a traditional department store to a warehouse store to e-commerce, and these shifts involve changes related to such things as product variety and the process for identifying and obtaining goods (**Conclusion 3-9**).

The federal statistical system collects two different types of price indices that can be used for deflation: the producer price index (PPI), which looks at changes in the prices of producer goods for a variety of inputs and at changes in margin prices for retail trade; and the consumer price index (CPI), which looks at changes in prices of consumer goods and is used to deflate sales revenue measures of output. Although the existing price indices provide a way of describing price changes that occur for the services and products provided by individual retail outlets, they do not capture the aggregate price changes that result as consumers move from one type of retail outlet to another. For example, the price indices do not reflect the change in the price and quality of retail services as consumers move from a traditional department store to a warehouse store to e-commerce, except when consumers move between outlets classified in different NAICS codes (**Conclusion 3-8**). Private-sector data could potentially be used to estimate the price effect of consumers moving between retail outlets (**Conclusion 3-11**) and provide more timely estimates of price changes in general (**Conclusion 3-12**).

Finally, employment is measured by estimating hours worked in the sector. The simple quantity of work hours should also be adjusted to reflect the different qualities of work provided by workers with different skill sets. In practice, this is done by looking at pay differences across groups of workers defined by difference in educational attainment, age, and gender. However, the retail transformation is substantially changing the workforce among some of the large retailers that are driving the biggest changes, with large increases in the number of workers with high-end programming and data analysis skills that support e-commerce (**Conclusion 3-10**). Private-sector data on payrolls could potentially be used to provide more timely estimates of quality-adjusted work hours (**Conclusion 3-12**).

BLS currently develops measures of employment and labor productivity in retail that focus on the retail sector as specifically defined by NAICS, use a sectoral output measure of nominal output that is deflated by the CPI, and reflect hours worked in retail establishments that are not adjusted for labor quality.

CONSIDERATIONS FOR CREATING A RETAIL SATELLITE ACCOUNT

A satellite account provides a framework to explore a specific aspect of the economy that is linked to the System of National Accounts while deviating in ways that help address important questions about that aspect of the economy. These deviations may involve grouping or valuing economic activities in ways that differ from those that the national accounts use or providing more detailed statistics than are provided in the national accounts (**Conclusion 4-1**).

There are several ways a retail satellite account might be defined to incorporate some of the related activities currently being integrated with retail services, such as wholesale, warehouse, and delivery functions. Including all establishments in these other industries would be feasible, but it would include many establishments with no relation to retail. Including only those establishments in these other industries that are part of retail enterprises would also be feasible, but that would exclude many relevant establishments simply because they are not owned by a retail enterprise. A "retail supporting" scope for a satellite account could include all establishments in transportation, warehousing, wholesale trade, and business services that serve retail trade firms, in addition to retail trade establishments themselves (**Conclusion 4-2**). If a retail satellite account's scope is limited to only those retail-supporting establishments that are part of larger retail enterprises, it will miss aspects of the sector's transformation that are taking place between rather than within firms.

The implementation of a retail-supporting satellite account would require estimating the portion of establishments in transportation, warehousing, wholesale trade, and business services that support retail (**Conclusion 4-4**). This split between retail-supporting and nonretail-supporting pieces would likely be different for the outputs of these sectors than for their labor input. It would be necessary to explore a variety of approaches for carrying out this split, including the use of alternative data sources. The input-output tables provide some information for estimating the split in output, but not the split in labor input. A collaborative effort across agencies could use microdata to explore issues related to a retail satellite account, including structural changes in firms and the role of auxiliary establishments (**Conclusion 4-3**).

The definition of the broader retail sector for a satellite account could be developed initially by using several definitions that are each simple to implement and that together provide lower and upper bounds for the included activities. A lower-bound definition could include all NAICS codes for retail establishments and for industries that are focused on supporting retail. An upper-bound definition could include all NAICS codes for industries that at least partially support retail. The range between these estimates would then indicate the potential benefit of developing careful approaches for splitting the input and output of industries that only partially support retail (**Conclusion 4-5**).

Several existing satellite accounts developed by the Bureau of Economic Analysis (BEA) may provide useful models for developing a retail satellite account, given the measurement challenges posed by the retail transformation. The digital economy satellite account includes e-commerce and digital services, which are both important aspects of the retail transformation. The health care satellite account involves a reconceptualization of health care spending, which might suggest novel ways to reflect the changing cost structure of retail. The outdoor recreation satellite account addresses the challenge of dividing up statistics from several industries to combine some of them in a new grouping that is useful to the field. The small business satellite account addresses the challenge of identifying establishments of different sizes, which may also be an important way to divide the data for the retail sector (**Conclusion 4-6**).

One approach to constructing a retail satellite account would be to create a central account with modules for experimentation and exploration.

This would allow it to reflect the current consensus in the central account while identifying areas where new information and further research are needed for a consensus to emerge. The modules might address issues such as alternative output measures and deflators; alternative aggregations and classifications of retail-related industries or inputs; experimental price indices that might better reflect new retail services; integrated analyses of retail products that cross the boundary between goods and services or between physical and digital goods; and alternative ways of measuring and allocating productivity gains.

RECOMMENDATIONS FOR A RETAIL SATELLITE ACCOUNT

The panel endorses the creation of a satellite account to study the transformation in retail trade. Such an account would be an appropriate and useful vehicle for BLS to use to study the impact on employment and productivity of the transformation in retail trade and to develop exploratory measures that describe that transformation (**Conclusion 5-1**).

Given the distribution of data and expertise across government agencies, BLS should develop a satellite account for an expanded retail trade sector in collaboration with BEA and Census. Such a team could be formed under the Evidence Based Policy Act to facilitate administrative and collaborative efforts (**Recommendation 1**).

The team developing the retail satellite account should solicit input and advice from industry and academia, with a special focus on collaboration with industry (**Conclusion 3-13**). Government statistics need input to ensure that the concepts being measured are relevant and keep up with the rapid pace of change in industry (**Recommendation 2**).

In implementing a satellite account, BLS and its partners should adopt an iterative and modular approach, starting with feasible options that draw upon the BEA industry account and the BLS-BEA integrated industry-level production account to see what insights these might provide about the sector and about feasible fixes. The modular approach should include a set of estimates in a central module, with a set of submodules to investigate important side questions or alternative measures and a set of studies to carry out over time to investigate relevant questions (**Recommendation 3**).

The satellite account should cover all retail and retail-supporting establishments, identifying these by combining available information from existing and enhanced data. The retail-supporting establishments should encompass all establishments supporting the distribution of retail goods to the consumer, but excluding their manufacturing and importing (**Recommendation 4**).

The satellite account should examine multiple measures of output, price deflators, and labor input in order to support comparisons that lead to informed decisions. Output measures should include gross sales and gross margins for trade industries, gross sales/revenues for other industries, and value-added for all industries. Deflators should include current margin deflators and new options that capture the changing characteristics of retail trade. Labor input measures should include simple hours worked and quality-adjusted hours worked to capture the changes in workforce quality. Modules should also be used to evaluate alternative approaches to estimating the split between retail-related and nonretail-related for both output and input (**Recommendation 5**).

The modules could also address more specialized issues that contribute to understanding the transition in retail trade, such as (1) international trade and global value chains, (2) digitization, (3) labor quality, and (4) providing real-time and subsector analyses. Over time, the central module would incorporate improvements developed in the submodules and in new data collection (**Recommendation 6**).

Given the errors introduced by the separate business registers used by BLS and Census, measures should be taken immediately to facilitate the reconciliation of business lists across agencies. This will require changes to be enacted by Congress or implemented by the Treasury Department to modify the relevant IRS regulations (**Recommendation 7**). BLS and Census should establish an interagency task force, potentially including other relevant agencies, to develop a plan for implementing a consolidated business register to use as the sample frame for all business surveys (**Recommendation 8**).

Developing a retail-related satellite account will require considerable effort to acquire and use data and to address data gaps in existing data. Individual projects include: Filling data gaps in the Economic Census and Economic Surveys that relate to the calculation of gross margins, value added, and the contribution of auxiliaries; identifying data to estimate the split in hours worked between retail-related and nonretail-related for retail-related service industries; correcting for differences in the numerator and denominator of productivity caused by the use of different business registers and classifications; and exploring the use of private-sector data to improve the timeliness and detail provided in the account. Some of these efforts are best accomplished by a team with access to the Census Bureau's economic microdata (**Recommendation 9**).

1

Introduction

Retail trade has experienced dramatic changes over the past several decades in the United States, with changes in the types of outlets where goods are sold, the nature of the transactions that provide goods to consumers, and the structure of retail operations behind the scenes. The recent changes include the rise of warehouse stores and e-commerce, and the further growth of import and large retail chains. These changes highlight and typify many aspects of the broader evolution of the economy as a whole in recent years—with the growing role of large firms and information technology—while taking place in a sector that directly serves the vast majority of the American population and provides substantial employment.

Despite the everyday experience of these dramatic changes in retail, there is concern that the most transformational aspects of those changes may not be captured well by the economic indicators relied on to understand the sector. In particular, the dynamic restructuring of retail should be accompanied by substantial improvements in productivity as retail firms innovate, but the sector's economic indicators do not tell a story of large productivity increases. This mismatch between everyday experience and economic indicators is more than an idle curiosity. It goes to the heart of our ability to understand the changes taking place in the U.S. economy and to develop appropriate policies in response.

In this context, the Bureau of Labor Statistics (BLS) asked the Committee on National Statistics (CNSTAT) of the National Academies of Sciences, Engineering, and Medicine to evaluate changes in the retail trade sector, assess measures of employment and labor productivity for the sector, and discuss the value of, and specifications for, a new satellite account that could measure retail-related employment and labor productivity in ways that would better capture the transformation. The request was motivated in part by shifts in the ways that warehouses, transportation services, and delivery services are now supporting retail, shifts that are not reflected in retail employment and labor productivity statistics because those statistics classify such services under industries separate from retail. The request was also motivated, more broadly, by a sense that the economic impacts of a range of retail innovations—highlighted by the growing and pervasive role information technology and e-commerce play in the sector—may not be well measured by the available indicators of retail employment and labor productivity.

To respond to this request from BLS, the National Academies formed the Panel on Measuring the Transformation of Retail Trade and Related Activities. The panel's statement of task is provided in Box 1-1.

The panel was just beginning its work to respond to the BLS request in 2020 when the COVID-19 crisis shocked the U.S. and world economies. This shock powerfully accelerated many of the longstanding retail trends that provided the motivation for the study, including the rise of e-commerce and the increasing role played by large retail chains, while pointedly demonstrating the sector's ability to innovate with the rapid evolution of shopping services and curbside delivery. The COVID-19 experience has provided a

---

BOX 1-1
Statement of Task

The Committee on National Statistics of the National Academies of Sciences, Engineering, and Medicine shall appoint an expert panel to review the issues related to measuring employment and productivity in retail-related industries for the Bureau of Labor Statistics (BLS) in the U.S. Department of Labor. The expert panel shall evaluate changes in the retail trade landscape and assess how they are impacting measures of employment and productivity in retail-related industries and determine if, and how, a satellite account can be designed to capture this retail transformation. The panel shall carefully review the existing measures as well as the methodological issues surrounding measurement of these concepts. As part of its information-gathering activities, the panel shall hold a public workshop to discuss the views of industry experts, academics doing work in related fields, and data users. The panel shall produce a consensus report, which shall include conclusions and recommendations for BLS on (1) the value and specifications for a satellite account for the retail-related sector, (2) ways to identify the proportion of output, employment, and hours outside of retail trade that are directed toward supporting retail trade, and (3) ways to maintain a retail-related satellite account.

dramatic example of the types of retail innovation that need to be reflected in the indicators of retail employment and labor productivity.

THE PANEL'S APPROACH

The panel's primary information-gathering activity consisted of holding a workshop that provided input from researchers, industry representatives, data users, and relevant statistical agencies. The workshop supplemented the panel's expertise related to the economics and statistics of the retail sector with additional expertise from economists who have studied the sector, government experts who understand the details of current government statistical programs, and industry representatives who are helping drive the sector's transformation.

The agenda for the workshop is provided in Appendix A. The workshop included sessions on the changes in retail, from the perspective of researchers and members of the industry; key measurement and data challenges for developing measures of employment and labor productivity; options for developing a satellite account for the retail sector; quality-adjusted prices for retail; uses of bottom-up measures in measuring employment and productivity for retail; and global value chains and the role of imports in the sector.

In deliberating on the workshop input, the panel took a broad approach to the options for a retail-related satellite account, considering both pragmatic immediate steps and aspirational longer-term goals and identifying ways to progress toward the aspirational goals by carrying out specific analyses and collecting additional data.

The next chapter provides an overview of the transformations occurring in the retail sector and the ways these are reflected in available indicators. Chapter 3 provides an overview of conceptual and data issues related to retail employment and labor productivity statistics, including brief descriptions of the government programs that collect relevant statistics. Chapter 4 discusses satellite accounts and key options that are relevant to establishing a satellite account for the retail sector. Finally, Chapter 5 provides the panel's recommendations for developing such a satellite account.

2

Transformation of the Retail Sector

This chapter describes recent changes in the retail sector, highlighting several important shifts since the 1990s in the way the sector is structured and the nature of the goods and services it provides. The chapter then considers these sectoral shifts and the way they extend or challenge the traditional definition of the retail sector. Finally, it turns to look at trends related to the retail sector from current statistical series to see what picture they provide of this sectoral transformation.

During the panel's workshop, four of the seven sessions provided an overview of important recent changes in the retail sector.[1] The first session considered the transformation from the perspective of researchers who study the sector. The second session considered the transformation from the perspective of industry representatives, focusing on participants who could provide a detailed understanding of the way the retail supply chain is being restructured. The sixth session looked at some of the trends in the sector that are revealed in analyses of firm-level data. Finally, the seventh session considered the importance of global value chains in the production of goods and services related to retail and the insights these provide about the way retail is changing.

---

[1]See Appendix A for the workshop agenda, including the panelists and moderators who participated in each session.

RECENT CHANGES IN THE RETAIL SECTOR

This section describes seven different but related changes in the retail sector, discussing each in turn. These changes capture the ways the sector is transforming that could be reflected in the government measures of the retail sector.

Collectively, these seven changes also illustrate a fundamental characteristic of the retail sector, which is its intensely dynamic nature. Without knowing in advance what new changes may appear in the future, it is a near-certainty that further changes of this magnitude will continue to appear to further challenge available measures of retail employment and labor productivity. So, while the seven changes discussed are important for the sector in the recent past and highlight important measurement challenges to address, they also illustrate the types of far-reaching change that will continue into the future in new and unexpected ways beyond the specific changes discussed here.

Rise of Warehouse Clubs and Supercenters

Since the 1990s, there has been a large shift toward warehouse clubs and supercenters (NAICS 452311)[2] at the expense of department stores (Hortaçsu and Syverson, 2015). Both formats are classified as general merchandise stores (NAICS 452), which represent one-fifth of total employment in the retail sector, 3.0 million out of 15.7 million employees.[3] Over the first two decades of this century, while employment in retail overall and in general merchandise stores stayed roughly constant,[4] there was a large shift in employment within general merchandise: department store employment decreased by 0.7 million while employment in general merchandise stores, including warehouse clubs and supercenters, increased by 0.9 million.[5] This shift moved department stores from 62 to 36 percent of employment in the

---

[2]Industry statistics in the United States are classified according to the North America Industry Classification System (NAICS). In the 2017 version of NAICS, there are 12 retail trade industries at the 3-digit level, 27 at the 4-digit level, and 66 at the 6-digit level. Warehouse clubs and supercenters are coded as 452311 in the 2017 release of NAICS and as 45291 in the 2012 release.

[3]3.0 million employees for general merchandise stores (NAICS 452) compared to 15.7 million for retail overall (NAICS 44-45), seasonally adjusted data for January 2020 [August 5, 2020] from https://data.bls.gov.

[4]Seasonally adjusted employment in January 2000 was 2.8 million for general merchandise stores and 15.2 million for retail overall.

[5]Seasonally adjusted employment in department stores (NAICS 4522) decreased from 1.73 million to 1.08 million from January 2000 to January 2020, while the corresponding employment in general merchandise stores, including warehouse clubs and supercenters (NAICS 4523), increased from 1.08 to 1.97 million.

general merchandise sector. The shift appears even more strikingly in sales figures, with department stores declining from 60 percent of total sales in the general merchandise sector in January 2000 to 18 percent in January 2020.[6] Warehouse clubs and supercenters are now the largest subindustry in general merchandise stores (NAICS 452).

The warehouse club and supercenter format moves some of the traditional functions of the warehouse into the store itself, providing inventory storage directly in the store. In addition, the shift moves toward a format that provides a lower level of customer service than is provided by traditional department stores and also includes food sales, which are not part of traditional department stores.

Rise of E-Commerce

The shift toward e-commerce is another important change in the retail sector (for a recent overview see Lafontaine and Sivadasan, forthcoming). Until recently, however, e-commerce remained a small part of retail overall, despite high growth rates. For example, nonstore retailers (NAICS 454) represented only 2.9 percent of total retail employment and only 7.9 percent of total retail sales in January 2010.[7] Total sales in nonstore retailers surpassed sales in general merchandise stores, including warehouse clubs and superstores, only in 2015.[8] According to the Census Bureau, e-commerce as a percentage of total sales grew from 0.6 percent in 1999 to 16.1 percent in the second quarter of 2020.[9]

As e-commerce has grown in recent years, it has become increasingly difficult to separate out the e-commerce portion of the industry. Most e-commerce could be identified within the nonstore retailer category as of 2013 (Hortaçsu and Syverson, 2015, p. 96), but e-commerce is becoming so pervasive that it is now not only difficult to clearly identify individual firms as predominantly e-commerce firms, but also often impossible to clearly classify individual retail sales as either e-commerce or not. The focus now for many retail firms is to adopt an "omni-channel" strategy, whereby they provide both e-commerce and in-store "channels" for customers to learn about and buy products. Customers frequently combine channels within a single purchase, sometimes reading online descriptions and reviews before

---

[6]Seasonally adjusted sales data for January 2000 and 2020. See https://www.census.gov/retail/mrts/historic_releases.html for department stores (2012 NAICS 4521).

[7]Seasonally adjusted employment of 0.416 million out of 14.4 million in January 2010 and seasonally adjusted sales of $27.3 billion out of $346 billion for the same month.

[8]See https://www.census.gov/retail/mrts/historic_releases.html.

[9]U.S. Census Bureau. (2020). *Census Bureau Provides Data on Fast-Growing Retail E-Commerce.* November 24. See https://www.census.gov/library/stories/2020/11/share-of-online-retail-sales-soaring.html.

inspecting a product in a store and purchasing it, but other times first seeing the product in a store and then later ordering it online after making comparisons across vendors.

The rise of e-commerce can be thought of as extending retail services in two different ways. First, e-commerce incorporates a set of warehouse services into the online store itself, providing customers with access to a vast range of inventory that goes far beyond the range of inventory that a brick-and-mortar store can physically stock. Second, e-commerce also extends the services provided by the retailer into a consumer's home, replacing some of the shopping and delivery services that consumers have until only recently provided for themselves. Providing these extended retail services has required the creation of substantial computing and demand analysis functions that are associated with the headquarters of large retailers and that produce substantial intangible assets that are essential to the success of these firms.

While e-commerce extends retail services, the digital technology that makes e-commerce possible also takes away a number of key retail services from the physical store itself, including providing information to customers about the products that are available, accepting the customer's payment to execute the purchase, and providing the product to the customer upon purchase. Those services are not only removed from the physical store, but also sometimes no longer directly provided by the retailer at all. For example, a freight company may contract with a retailer to manage inventory, interact with customers to execute purchases, and deliver products, operating under the retailer's own brand.

The section further below on responses to the COVID-19 crisis describes the substantial acceleration of e-commerce that has occurred in response to the pandemic.

Digital Transformation of Retail Goods

Digital technology has not only allowed e-commerce but also transformed the form of many retail goods themselves. Books, music, and video provide clear examples of this transformation, with products that used to be sold as physical goods now largely transformed into digital downloads that may be either sold or rented. Of course, the renting of retail products has existed for a long time, notably for car leasing and formal wear. However, digital technology has made it increasingly feasible to expand the rental markets for other consumer goods, such as a much broader range of clothing (e.g., Rent the Runway).

A few statistics provide an illustration of the range of these changes. Revenue from e-books and downloaded audio books totaled $3.25 billion in 2019, representing 12.5 percent of total publishing industry revenue, up from 7.3 percent in 2015. Between 2015 and 2019, e-book and downloaded audio book revenue increased by 61 percent.[10] Expenditures on video and audio streaming and rental, as a proportion of total expenditures on video and audio, have increased from 22.3 percent in 2000 to 32.5 percent in 2010 to 66.5 percent in 2019.[11] For comparison, expenditures on motor vehicle rental and leasing as a proportion of total expenditures on new motor vehicles, including sales, rentals, and leasing, have fluctuated between 13 and 23 percent since 1994 without a clear trend, after increasing from below 2 percent in the 1980s.[12]

Imports of Retail Goods and Services

Imports of retail goods and services are also transforming the sector. For example, four large retailers (Walmart, Target, Home Depot, and Lowe's) accounted for almost 10 percent of U.S. imports by volume in 2018.[13] These large firms import directly, providing their own import distribution centers. Some product categories—such as toys, furniture, clothing, and electronics—are heavily dependent on imports. Imports of consumer goods totaled $1.19 trillion in 2007, having grown 3.7 times from the value of $319 billion in 1992 (Smith, 2019).[14] Consumer imports in 2007 represented almost a quarter of total retail and food services sales of $4.4 trillion.[15]

Given the complexity of global supply chains, it can be difficult to identify the domestic and imported portions of a good's value, whether it comes directly from a domestic or foreign manufacturer. Complex products, such as motor vehicles and consumer electronics, often include components sourced from several different countries. In addition, the value of many imports includes intellectual property, which may actually be owned by the importing U.S. firm. Despite the complexity of many products, a number

---

[10] Revenue figures provided by the American Association of Publishers. See https://publishers.org/news/aap-statshot-annual-report-book-publishing-revenues-up-slightly-to-25-93-billion-in-2019.

[11] BEA, nominal Personal Consumption Expenditures, comparing nominal expenditures on video and audio streaming and rental with total nominal expenditures on video and audio streaming and rental along with recording media. Calculated from the underlying detail tables for Personal Consumption Expenditures, see https://apps.bea.gov/iTable/index_nipa.cfm.

[12] BEA, nominal Personal Consumption Expenditures, comparing nominal expenditures on motor vehicle leasing, motor vehicle rental, and new motor vehicles. Calculated from the underlying detail tables for Personal Consumption Expenditures, see https://apps.bea.gov/iTable/index_nipa.cfm.

[13] See https://www.joc.com/maritime-news/top-100-us-importer-and-exporter-rankings-2018_20190530.html, cited by Dominic Smith at the panel's workshop.

[14] Both figures reported in 2007 dollars.

[15] See https://www.census.gov/retail/mrts/www/mrtssales92-present.xls.

of international organizations and researchers have developed global input-output estimates of their global value chains.[16]

In addition to imports of the retail goods for sale in the United States, some portion of retail services can also be outsourced by retail firms. For example, L.L. Bean carries out much of its back-office work in Costa Rica.[17]

Role of Large Firms in the Retail Transformation

The four changes previously mentioned have been driven by national and regional multi-unit retail firms, which lead productivity growth in the industry and represent most of the sector's growth in sales and employment (Foster et al., 2016). Sales of the eight largest retail firms as a percentage of all retail sales rose from 11.7 percent to 19.5 percent from 1997 to 2012.[18] Single-unit retail firms still account for roughly 60 percent of retail establishments, but only 30 percent of retail sales.[19]

Large firms pose a challenge to developing statistics by industry, since their level of integration indicates clear economies of scale and scope that go across their divisions. Fundamentally, this means that some inputs—at a minimum, each firm's management—are contributing to multiple outputs in a way that cannot easily be apportioned for statistics or reproduced by single-unit firms. For firms that have retail divisions in addition to other divisions—such as manufacturing, warehousing, or transportation—it is hard to appropriately attribute the common inputs that are contributing to the retail portion of the firm.

Despite the increasing role played by large firms over the past several decades, the digital systems that have become pervasive over this same period now allow retailers to outsource many retail functions to other providers, including customer interaction and order fulfillment. These systems increasingly allow any retailer to reproduce the same quality and speed in customer interaction and order fulfillment that a company like Amazon can provide. This suggests that the transformation that has been driven by

---

[16] See work by the Organisation for Economic Co-operation and Development with the World Trade Organization, https://www.oecd.org/sti/ind/measuring-trade-in-value-added.htm; by the Global Trade Analysis Project, see https://www.gtap.agecon.purdue.edu/; and by the World Input-Output Database, http://www.wiod.org/home.

[17] Cited by Marshall Reinsdorf at the panel's workshop.

[18] Census Bureau, Economic Census of Retail Trade: Establishment and Firm Size (Including Legal Form of Organization), 1997 Economic Census, Retail Trade, Subject Series, Issued October 2000, EC97R44S-SZ, Table 6, page 197, see https://www2.census.gov/library/publications/economic-census/1997/retail-trade/97r44-sz.pdf, for 1997; and https://data.census.gov/cedsci/table?q=EC1244&tid=ECNSIZE2012.EC1244SSSZ6&hidePreview=true for 2012.

[19] John Haltiwanger at the panel's workshop.

the large retail firms over the past couple decades is now being extended in a way that smaller retailers can use, with implications throughout the entire sector.

Increased Product Variety

A number of changes in the retail sector already discussed have contributed to a general change reflected across the sector in making more products available to consumers and providing new retail services to help consumers navigate and take advantage of growing product variety. This can be seen in the sheer number of products offered at warehouse clubs and supercenters, which has increased again with the rise of e-commerce, where nonstore retailers can offer a huge range of products beyond the limits of a physical store. At the same time, inventory management software and online search and recommendations systems allow consumers to identify and obtain specific products from the vast array offered for sale, powerfully extending the service that retailers have always provided in presenting and organizing products for consumers to consider purchasing. These services include the ability of consumers to easily compare prices and customer reviews and to have their purchases delivered directly and quickly to their homes, making it possible for them to access a larger variety of products while simultaneously reducing shopping time, travel costs, and prices.

Changes in Response to COVID-19

This project was carried out virtually while the United States, along with much of the rest of the world, was struggling to find a successful response to the COVID-19 pandemic. That context highlighted changes that the pandemic had already brought to the retail sector and might bring in the future, beyond the temporary closure of many retail stores during the initial response, which in many cases may become permanent.

Dramatic changes in e-commerce occurred during the first two quarters of the COVID-19 crisis. E-commerce sales increased by 31.9 percent from the first quarter to the second quarter of 2020, and e-commerce sales in the third quarter of 2020 were 36.7 percent larger than in the third quarter of 2019.[20] E-commerce in the second and third quarters of 2020 represented 16.1 percent and 14.3 percent of total U.S. retail sales, respectively, compared to 11.8 percent in the first quarter of 2020. Relatedly, there has been a surprising surge in applications for new businesses during the COVID-19 crisis, dominated by an increase in applications for nonstore retailers.[21]

---

[20] See https://www.census.gov/retail/mrts/www/data/pdf/ec_current.pdf.
[21] See https://www.census.gov/econ/bfs/projects.html.

These patterns suggest that the COVID-19 crisis has accelerated the long-run trend toward a greater role for e-commerce in retail trade.

HOW RECENT RETAIL CHANGES RELATE TO THE BASIC DEFINITION OF THE SECTOR

The different changes that have occurred in the retail sector sometimes raise the question of whether the transformed activities should still be classified as belonging to retail. This question is raised with particular urgency by e-commerce, where a growing number of firms now provide some aspects of retail services without identifying themselves as retail firms. Does a freight company that subcontracts with a retailer to provide customer service and order fulfillment services effectively become a retail establishment in some sense? The digital transformation of some traditional retail goods poses similar questions. Should books or videos that are now provided as digital downloads or as part of a larger subscription service be included as part of the retail sector? We discuss these two questions in turn.

Relation of Retail to Other Industries

The potential difficulty in deciding whether some firms belong to the retail classification leads to a consideration of the essential characteristics that define the retail sector. Retail is often identified as facing the final consumer and distributing "retail-like products" without transforming them. The definition used by NAICS notes that retail provides services that are "incidental to the sale of merchandise" and that retail "is the final step in the distribution of merchandise."[22] The NAICS definition further notes that "the buying of goods for resale is a characteristic of retail trade establishments that particularly distinguishes them from establishments in the agriculture, manufacturing, and construction industries."

Thus, a farm, manufacturer, or housing developer that sells directly to the public is not considered to be a retailer because each of these businesses produces what it sells, rather than buying products for resale. Wholesale trade is also distinguished from retail trade, because wholesalers "are not usually organized to serve the general public." The NAICS definition notes that "dealers of durable nonconsumer goods, such as farm machinery and heavy-duty trucks, are included in wholesale trade even if they often sell these products in single units" and even though they are often sold to the final (business) purchaser. The NAICS definition also provides examples of "incidental" services that are sometimes provided by retailers, including

---

[22] See https://www.census.gov/naics/?input=44&chart=2017&details=44.

"the provision of after-sales services, such as repair and installation" in the cases of "new automobile dealers, electronics and appliance stores, and musical instrument and supplies stores." Some processing activities are also considered "incidental" to the retailing function such as "optical goods stores that do in-store grinding of lenses, and meat and seafood markets." Thus, the existing definitions identify retailers as those who purchase goods for resale to the general public with limited transformation of those goods.

Traditionally, a relatively stable wholesale sector moved goods between manufacturers and retailers without directly interfacing with final consumers. The warehousing sector stored goods in the transition from manufacturer to final consumer, and the transportation sector moved goods between manufacturer, wholesaler, retailer, and final consumer. As noted above, large retailers today often directly provide wholesale services (including direct importing), along with related warehousing and transportation functions. Retailers may outsource some of the services related to retail, such as customer service or order fulfillment, either to specialized firms operating invisibly under the umbrella of the retailer's brand or to other retailers like Amazon. In some cases, a retailer may outsource order fulfillment to a manufacturer, who may deliver directly to the consumer without the retailer ever taking possession of the good and holding it in inventory.

As a result of these transformations, large retailers have often added functions performed by the wholesale, warehousing, and transportation industries, and they may also have outsourced some retail services to specialized providers. Nevertheless, they still largely provide the defining function of purchasing goods for resale to the general public with limited transformation. In that sense, the traditional definition of retail trade still applies to large retailers, even after these transformations, as much as it applies to traditional single-unit retailers that use the wholesale, warehousing, and transportation sectors in the traditional ways. However, the internal cost structure of large and small retailers and the functions provided by their employees are likely to be quite different. A large retailer may obtain goods at a lower cost directly from the manufacturer (domestic or foreign), but then provide various wholesale, warehousing, and transportation services internally that a traditional single-unit retailer would have to pay for. At the same time, a large retailer may outsource some traditional retail services, like customer service, that a traditional single-unit retailer provides directly. These different arrangements of purchased and produced services need to be reflected to provide meaningful comparisons of employment and productivity across large and small retailers that can apply as the sector continues to evolve.

CONCLUSION 2-1: The traditional definition of retail trade applies to the large retailers that have become increasingly important over the past few decades as well as it applies to more traditional small retailers. However, the cost structures of these two types of firms can be quite different. Large retailers often provide wholesale, warehousing, and transportation services directly, whereas small retailers usually purchase these services. In addition, large retailers sometimes outsource some traditional retail services, such as customer service and order fulfilment, whereas small retailers usually provide these services directly. Defining retail output as the quantity of goods sold will understate the contribution of retailers that provide high levels of service.

Range of Goods and Services Included in the Retail Sector

One aspect of the transformation on the goods side involves digital versions of products, such as books and videos, that were previously provided physically. In cases where the digital versions are provided by a retailer (such as Amazon) as well as a publisher, the standard retail definition would classify the sales as occurring in the retail sector, recognizing that goods can be considered to be intangible (Reinsdorf and Slaughter, 2009). Of course, if the digital books were sold by the publisher, the sale would be counted within the information industry (NAICS 51), but that is no different from other sales occurring directly from manufacturers. However, if digital goods are leased rather than sold, then they no longer fall under the definition of retail, instead moving to rental and leasing services (NAICS 532), which includes automobile leasing and various other types of leasing, such as formal wear, home health equipment, and office machinery.

On the retail services side, e-commerce has replaced some of the shopping and delivery services that consumers have until recently provided for themselves (Mandel, 2017). This type of shift is not novel; in earlier periods, deliveries of this type were sometimes standard, as when retailers provided home delivery of milk. However, this shifting in the types of services provided by the retail sector can make it difficult to interpret changes that are occurring in measured employment and productivity. Specifically, the extra services can produce an increase in employment and therefore possibly suggest a decrease in productivity unless the output measure recognizes that a greater level of service is being provided, as reflected in the significant reduction in unpaid shopping hours reported by the American Time Use Survey.[23]

These two changes, which involve shifts from activities inside the traditional retail definition to activities outside that definition or vice

---

[23] See https://www.bls.gov/tus.

versa—movement of some products from sales to leasing, and shifts in the direct labor provided by consumers—underline potential challenges to collecting meaningful statistics during a period of sector change. These types of changes are not novel and occur in other sectors as well as retail, but their effects may be extensive enough in retail that it is worth the extra effort to understand their role in affecting employment and productivity. Since both involve shifts related to what is included in the retail category, understanding the effects of these changes on employment and productivity would require analyses that combine or compare information from inside and outside the traditional retail category.

> **CONCLUSION 2-2:** In cases where the recent transformation in the retail sector has shifted some retail services outside the traditional definition of the sector (e.g., by moving from sales to leasing of some products like clothes or movies) or brought some services into retail that were formerly outside the traditional definition (e.g., by delivering purchases that consumers previously purchased at a store), an understanding of the employment and productivity effects of the changes will require analyses that compare services inside and outside the retail sector.

Beyond these examples, there are further expansions in the types of goods and services offered by large retailers that go well beyond the traditional retail sector, such as the provision of cloud computing by Amazon and of consumer health services by Walmart. Under the standard NAICS classification system, these products would be classified in other industries (NAICS 518 and 621, respectively). The only difficulty that might arise concerns the extent to which large firms operating in multiple industries necessarily comingle work related to those different industries, at a minimum with respect to the contribution of the firms' management. This situation necessarily requires some approximation in allocating inputs to different industries, though that is a challenge throughout the economic statistical system and is not specific to the retail transformation.

THE RETAIL TRANSFORMATION AS SEEN IN EXISTING STATISTICAL SERIES

As a starting point in considering the statistical challenge of portraying and understanding the retail transformation, Figure 2-1 illustrates the sector's labor productivity as measured by three different statistical series. In each case, the series looks at the average annual change in labor productivity over the 21-year period from 1997 to 2018, where labor productivity

24   A SATELLITE ACCOUNT TO MEASURE THE RETAIL TRANSFORMATION

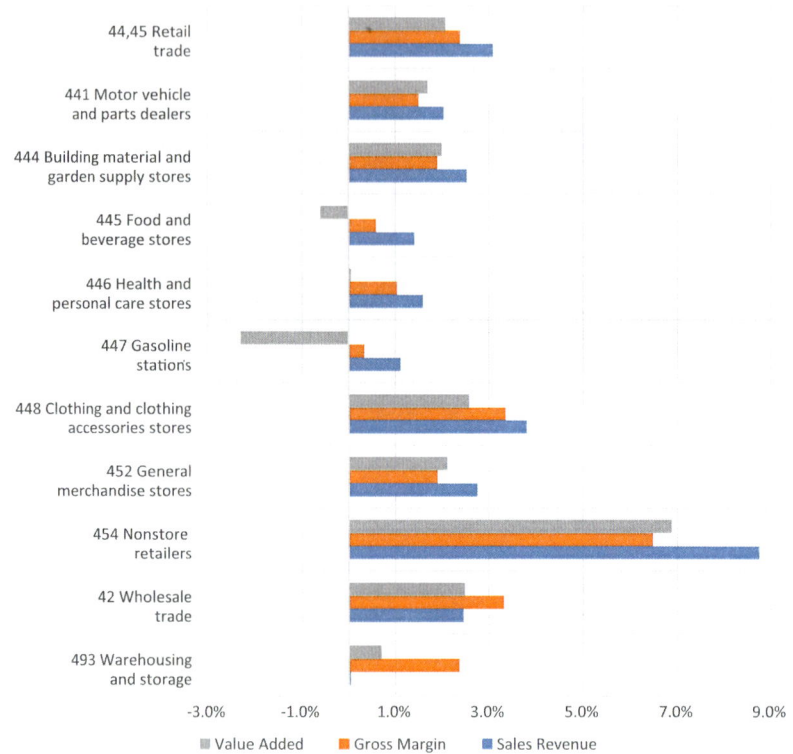

FIGURE 2-1 Average annual change in labor productivity, 1997-2018, by type of output measure.
SOURCES: Output measured by sales revenue from U.S. Bureau of Labor Statistics (BLS), Division of Industry Productivity Studies. Labor productivity calculated by dividing change in output by change in hours worked, using hours data from BLS (BLS data from https://www.bls.gov/lpc/lpc_by_industry_and_measure.xlsx using the "Output" and "Hours" fields for the sale revenue and hours indices, respectively). Output measured by gross margin and value added from U.S. Bureau of Economic Analysis, Industry Data webpage (using the "Chain-Type Quantity Index" for both gross output and value added). All series provided in Appendix B.

is defined as the real output in the sector divided by the hours worked.[24] The three series define retail output in different ways: (1) as total sales revenue; (2) as the difference between sales revenue and the cost of goods

---

[24] Appendix B, which contains the underlying data, also breaks the series at 2007, which shows the slowdown in retail labor productivity growth that occurred from the first decade (1997-2007) to the second (2007-2018).

sold (gross margin); and (3) as the difference between sales revenue and the cost of all purchased inputs (value added), with nominal values deflated by appropriate price indices in each case. Labor productivity growth rates are provided for the retail sector overall, along with the major three-digit retail subindustries, and they are provided as well for two other sectors for comparison: wholesale trade and warehousing.

The data underlying these series are discussed in Chapter 3, but the focus in this chapter is simply on comparisons of the qualitative picture of the sector that emerges from the changes discussed above and the quantitative picture that emerges from the different statistical series

The changes experienced by retail over the past few decades suggest that the sector is highly competitive and is undergoing substantial change and reorganization. As discussed earlier, the changes described involve warehouse clubs and superstores (a part of general merchandise, NAICS 452), e-commerce (concentrated in NAICS 454 in earlier periods and expanded to NAICS 493 in more recent periods), digital goods, imports, and large firms, along with some more recent changes brought about by COVID-19.

By contrast, the three statistical series describe a sector where annual labor productivity growth averaged 2.1 to 3.1 percent per year over the two decades from 1997 to 2018. This growth in labor productivity was not substantially different from the 2.1 percent growth in labor productivity for the nonfarm business sector over this period.[25] Despite the similarity across the three estimates, the cumulative differences in these growth rates over the 21-year period are substantial, with the sales revenue measure reflecting a cumulative labor productivity increase of 92.5 percent, compared to the 56.5 percent increase that emerges from the value-added measure.[26] The range across these three figures reflects meaningfully different pictures of the labor productivity growth in the retail sector.

The one retail subindustry that clearly stands out for its labor productivity performance is the nonstore sector, where labor productivity was more than twice as large as for the retail sector as a whole. However, for general merchandise stores, which saw substantial restructuring in the decline of department stores and the rise of warehouse clubs and supercenters, productivity changes look no different than for the rest of the retail sector in the three statistical series.

Another observation of note in Figure 2-1 is the cases where there is a clear divergence in the picture provided by the different statistical series: Food and beverage stores (NAICS 445) and gasoline stations (NAICS 447)

---

[25] Haver Analytics database, nonfarm business sector, real output per hour of all persons, Bureau of Labor Statistics, annualized percent growth based on annual data, 1997-2018.

[26] See Appendix B.

both show labor productivity falling when measured using value added, but rising when using sales revenue or gross margin. Similarly, health and personal care stores (NAICS 446) show zero labor productivity when measured using value added, compared to rising productivity when measured using sales revenue or gross margin.

There is no way for the other changes discussed above to be directly reflected in Figure 2-1. The subindustry breakdowns do not align with changes in digital goods and services, imports, or the role of large firms.

Table 2-1 provides several indicators besides labor productivity that show the extent of some of the changes discussed in the retail sector. The

TABLE 2-1 Several Indicators of the Retail Transformation, 1997-2019 (percentage)

	1997	2002	2007	2012	2017	2019
Warehouse and supercenter share of total retail sales	4.6	7.3	9.3	10.9	10.8	10.6
Nonstore retailer share of total retail sales	5.1	6.1	7.7	9.5	12.5	14.6
Employment share in firms with <500 employees		42.9	39.0	35.9	35.2	
Employment share in firms with 10,000+ employees		44.6	49.7	52.3	53.5	
Share of total retail sales for 8 largest retail firms	11.7	15.3	17.5	19.5		
E-commerce share of sales:						
Music and video			12.3	41.2	76.5	
Books and magazines			9.1	22.1	41.1	
Computers and software			18.7	30.3	32.9	
Food and beverages			0.2	0.7	0.9	

SOURCES: Sales data from BLS, https://www.bls.gov/lpc/lpc_by_industry_and_measure.xlsx, using the Value of Production field for NAICS 45231 (General merchandise, including warehouses and supercenters), NAICS 454 (Nonstore retailers), and NAICS 44, 45 (Retail trade). Employment data from Census Bureau, Statistic of US Business (SUSB), https://www.census.gov/programs-surveys/susb/data/tables.html, for Retail Trade. Revenue share of 8 largest firms from Census Bureau, Economic Census of Retail Trade, https://www.census.gov/programs-surveys/economic-census/data/tables.html. E-commerce share of sales calculated in Hortaçsu and Syverson, 2015, Table 1, "by dividing the sum of the product category's e-commerce sales within and outside Electronic Shopping and Mail-Order Houses (ESMOH) by the sum of total ESMOH sales of the product and total sales of the product's corresponding retail industry." Chad Syverson generously provided the underlying data points for the series. The 2012 value for computers and software is missing in the series and is calculated in the table as the average of 2011 and 2013.

first pair of figures shows the shift in the share of total retail sales in the subset of general merchandise stores that includes warehouse clubs and supercenters (NAICS 45231) and in nonstore retailers (NAICS 454). In both cases, the share of total retail sales in these types of outlets more than doubles over two decades, and the shift is large in relation to overall retail sales. The second set of figures shows the shift in the employment share in small (< 500 employees) and large (10,000+ employees) firms, with a shift of 8 percentage points in overall retail employment from small to large firms over a 15-year period. It also shows the shift in revenue of the largest eight retail firms over an earlier (but overlapping) 15-year period. Finally, the third set of figures shows estimates of the e-commerce share of sales in different product categories over a single decade, with substantial shifts to e-commerce in some product categories—music and video, books and magazines—and very small shifts in others, especially in food and beverages.

3

Measuring Retail Employment and Labor Productivity

This chapter discusses the task of measuring retail employment and productivity, addressing both the conceptual elements that need to be measured and the available data for doing so. Inevitably, the available data fall short of capturing the concepts, which leads to the discussion in the next chapter of possible ways of addressing those shortfalls in the context of a retail satellite account.

As a starting point for discussion, this chapter first clarifies two high-level concepts essential to measuring productivity and its components: *output* (including price deflators) and *input*. It then considers the definition of the retail sector, which structures the way data related to retail are collected, expanding on the relevant concepts and the data provided by U.S. federal statistical programs to measure output, including deflators, and employment. The chapter ends with a discussion of alternative data sources.

The concepts and data presented here derive from two main sources: documentation provided by the U.S. federal statistical agencies and the information-gathering workshop organized by the panel. The panel's workshop included three sessions related to measurement issues. The workshop's third session focused on key measurement and data challenges, with particular attention to the data collected and the measures produced by the Bureau of Labor Statistics (BLS), the U.S Census Bureau, and the Bureau of Economic Analysis (BEA). The workshop's fifth session focused on quality-adjusted prices, a particularly difficult measurement issue related to deflation of output. The sixth session discussed improvements in the measurement of retail trade productivity that might be gained using microdata from the statistical agencies. Beyond those three sessions, the workshop's other sessions prompted a number of exchanges on the conceptual and data issues related to measuring retail employment and labor productivity.

MEASURING RETAIL EMPLOYMENT AND LABOR PRODUCTIVITY: THE HIGH-LEVEL TASK

The project focuses on the concepts and data needed to measure employment and labor productivity in the retail sector. This scope immediately raises questions about the ways such terms as "employment," "labor productivity," and "retail sector" should be defined. Answering those questions is the task of this chapter, and it is also the main focus of government economic statistics programs that must implement data-gathering processes to produce a set of measures of the economy.

A key point to note is that the productivity concept at issue is *labor* productivity, not multifactor productivity. Labor productivity concerns the amount of output produced per unit of labor input. At heart, this involves the division of industry output by labor input, once the appropriate measures have been defined. Box 3-1 summarizes the current labor productivity measures produced by BLS for the trade industries (retail and wholesale) and retail-related services. For these industries, the output measure currently used by BLS is gross sales deflated with a price index. That is, the sales figure is adjusted to convert dollars to a base year, in order to remove apparent changes in output that are actually due to price changes. Input is measured as hours worked.

Alternative approaches to measuring labor productivity for retail-related industries also use the equation shown in Box 3-1 but may define output (deflated using an appropriate deflator) as *gross margin* (sales revenue minus cost of goods sold), *sectoral output*[1] (gross output minus all inputs originating from firms within the industry being measured), or *value added* (gross output minus the value of all inputs originating as the output of other firms).

BLS measures labor productivity by deflating detailed revenues with corresponding price indexes, using either its own Consumer Price Index (CPI) or Producer Price Index (PPI) or else Merchant Wholesale Deflators from BEA.

BLS determines the revenue obtained from specific product classifications within each industry. Revenues for detailed product classes are deflated with corresponding price indexes. For about 97 percent of retail sales, BLS uses price indexes from CPI. For about 3 percent of the sales the Bureau uses a PPI, because pricing data for those products or services are not

---

[1] The BLS labor productivity measures for the manufacturing sector, individual manufacturing industries, and NIPA-level nonmanufacturing industries are calculated under a sectoral output approach.

> **BOX 3-1**
> **Labor Productivity for Trade-Related Industries:**
> **How It Is Measured by the Bureau of Labor Statistics**
>
> *Representation*: Business establishments in the United States, by industry (NAICS code).
> *When released*: Up to 8 months after the close of the reference year for preliminary values; up to 20 months after the close of the reference year for revised values.
> *Key variables*: Labor productivity; output; hours worked; and implicit price deflator.
> *Level of detail*: 2-, 3-, and 4-digit NAICS codes, with some 5- and 6-digit detail.
> *Measurement*: Annual productivity growth is derived as the annual percentage change in real output minus the annual percentage change in hours worked:
>
> $$(DO_t/DO_{t-1}) - (H_t/H_{t-1})$$
>
> where O_t represents output (sales, revenue, or value of shipments) from the Census Bureau's annual (revised values) and monthly or quarterly (preliminary values) economic surveys at time t plus revenue from the Census Bureau's Nonemployer Statistics at time t. $DO_t = O_t/D_t$ where D_t is a deflator (or price index) that converts dollars to a base year to remove any change in output due to price changes. H_t represents input (hours worked) at time t from BLS. (See Box 3-7.)

available from the CPI. For services, BLS employs a mix of PPIs and CPIs, using a larger portion of the former depending on the industry. For wholesale output, BLS uses PPIs for the manufacturers' sales branches and offices and merchant wholesale deflators from BEA. For industries for which BLS possesses revenue detail from the Economic Census (conducted every 5 years) to break up the annual sales, BLS applies available product- or service-specific deflators to the detailed portion of the total revenue. When the Bureau does not have the revenue detail, as for several services industries, it uses the total-industry deflator from PPI.[2] Alternatives would use a price deflator appropriate for the selected output measure.

The input measure currently used by BLS to estimate labor productivity is hours worked. Alternative formulations adjust hours worked for differences in labor composition (typically, education or skill). An example of a potential alternative formulation[3] is used by BLS in its formulation of multifactor productivity, as described next.

---

[2] From e-mails with Jenny Rudd, BLS, December 14-16, 2020.
[3] Another potential alternative way of accounting for labor composition is used by BLS/BEA in their joint Industry-Level Production Account.

Multifactor productivity involves multiple inputs in addition to labor—including various forms of capital and other purchased inputs such as energy, materials, or purchased services. In addition, the BLS multifactor productivity measure adjusts hours worked to account for differences in labor composition. As described in BLS (2020):

> At the major sector level, measures of hours worked are supplemented to account for changes in so-called 'labor composition'. This is a measure of the overall level of skill of the labor force. To compute the change in labor composition, the labor force is sorted into types of workers, defined by combinations of age, education, and gender. For each of these worker types (a.k.a. 'cells'), total hours worked and median hourly wage are calculated in each year. Wages are assumed to be a proxy for worker skill, with more skilled workers receiving greater compensation.
>
> The hours and wage data are used to calculate each type of worker's share of total wages. The labor composition adjustment is calculated as the difference between the percent change in total hours worked and the weighted sum of the percent changes of hours worked by each age/education/gender worker type.

Because multifactor productivity involves multiple inputs, computations are more complex. This report does not address the additional conceptual and data issues related to measuring multifactor productivity.

DEFINING THE RETAIL SECTOR

This discussion starts with the last of the three terms that need to be defined—"retail sector"—because of its centrality to the motivation for the project. Specifically, the project seeks to answer the question, Has the transformation in retail affected the definition of the sector in ways that would require a different, perhaps broader, definition of the sector? The statement of task for the project asks about the creation of a satellite account that could address a "retail-related" sector that would go beyond the businesses included in retail alone.

This section first considers how the definition of industries in economic data affects the ability to identify a retail-related sector. It then turns to an important practical problem in the way industry classification is carried out in the United States across multiple statistical agencies.

Defining Retail-Related Establishments in Federal Data

One of the key organizing frameworks for federal economic data is provided by the North American Industry Classification System (NAICS), which classifies establishments in a hierarchical coding system according to their primary activity. Box 3-2 provides more detail about NAICS. NAICS was implemented in 1997 to replace the Standard Industrial Classification

---

**BOX 3-2
Measuring the Economy
The North American Industry Classification System (NAICS)**

The Great Depression of the 1930s spawned many new federal mechanisms for tracking the economy. One of them was the Standard Industrial Classification (SIC) system, developed when manufacturing was the dominant industry. While there were many modifications to the SIC over the years, by the 1990s it was clear that major shifts in the American economy mandated major change in how its industries were classified. The result: the North American Industry Classification System (NAICS), adopted in 1997.[a]

NAICS is now the standard used by federal statistical agencies in the United States, as well as those in Canada and Mexico, to classify business establishments, that is, economic units at a single location that produce and/or sell goods or services. The classification is valuable for collecting, analyzing, and publishing statistical data related to the business economy. Revisions to NAICS are considered every 5 years in calendar years ending with 2 and 7 through international collaborations. For 2022, the main items under consideration were released for comment in the *Federal Register* in February 2020.[b] Of particular relevance to the study of retail trade are the discussions in sections III and IV concerning NAICS 454111, Electronic Shopping, and NAICS 519130, Internet Publishing and Broadcasting and Web Search Portals. These codes delineate industries based on mode of delivery, the internet, rather than by product as most NAICS codes within the retail and wholesale sectors are delineated.

Under NAICS, establishments that have similar production processes are classified in the same industry, and support establishments are designated as auxiliaries during the classification process. Business establishments are identified with individual locations and may be part of a larger firm ("enterprise") that may have establishments working in a number of different industries. Each statistical agency implements the classification of business establishments based on its own available data.[c]

The major NAICS designations of interest to this project are these three sectors: retail trade (NAICS 44-45), wholesale trade (NAICS 42), and transportation and warehousing (NAICS 48-49); as well as the more detailed codes within those sectors. Elements of other sectors may also be included in the analysis to fully account for the transformation of retail trade.

---

[a] See http://www.incontext.indiana.edu/2002/july-aug02/details.asp.
[b] See https://www.federalregister.gov/documents/2020/02/26/2020-03797/2017-north-american-industry-classification-system-naics-updates-for-2022-update-of-statistical.
[c] See https://www.census.gov/eos/www/naics/2017NAICS/2017_NAICS_Manual.pdf (p. 3); and https://www.census.gov/eos/www/naics/history/history.html, third file on NAICS classification memos.

System (SIC), which classified establishments by sector using different concepts, such as production- or demand-based definitions.

A key difference between the SIC and NAICS classifications is in their treatment of auxiliary establishments. As Fort and Klimek (2018, p. 8) explain,

> Auxiliary establishments are defined as those establishments primarily serving other establishments of the same enterprise. Examples of auxiliary establishments include management, warehousing, data processing, and R&D. Under SIC, auxiliary establishments were classified in the primary industry of the establishments that they served. In contrast, NAICS classifies these establishments in a number of different industries and sectors, depending upon the types of services the establishments actually provide.

Hence, under NAICS, additional information needs to be used to identify whether an establishment is an auxiliary that primarily supports retail trade.

The 1992 Economic Census, the last such census that relied solely on SIC classifications, showed more than 840,000 auxiliary employees assigned to retail trade out of a total of 18 million retail trade employees. Also in 1992, BLS payroll data showed 13 million retail trade employees. In 1997, the Economic Census collected data with sufficient detail so that it could be categorized under both SIC and NAICS. That year the number of retail trade employees fell to 13 million, close to the count from BLS payroll data. Today, under the NAICS system, the auxiliary employees who had been listed in retail trade under the SIC classifications are most likely to have been moved to one or more of the following sectors or subsectors: Management of Companies and Enterprises; Administrative Support, Waste Management and Remediation Services; Warehousing and Storage; Computer Systems Design and Related Services; and Accounting, Tax Preparation, Bookkeeping and Payroll Services.[4]

Ding and colleagues (2020, p. 1) illustrated the impact of auxiliaries on the manufacturing sector, observing that

> firms with in-house professional service establishments are larger, grow faster, are more likely to survive, and are more likely to open plants in other sectors than firms without such plants. These trends motivate a model of within-firm structural transformation in which non-manufacturing workers complement physical production, and where physical input price reductions induce firms to reallocate toward services.

The changes in the retail trade sector discussed in the preceding chapter suggest that a broader definition of the sector than provided by NAICS

---

[4] See http://www.incontext.indiana.edu/2002/july-aug02/details.asp.

might be required to be able to understand the shifts that are occurring. In particular, the restructuring that started first with the warehouse clubs and superstores and then moved on to e-commerce has begun to blur the lines between the retail industry and several other sectors, including wholesale trade, warehousing and storage, different types of transportation, and some other types of business services.

The ability to analyze these changes in an integrated way is directly affected by the structure of the economic data in the U.S. federal statistical system and, therefore, by the NAICS classification.

CONCLUSION 3-1: Given the structure of economic data in the U.S. federal statistical system, a study of the retail-related sector will require identifying those North American Industry Classification System codes that can be defined as either retail related or partially retail related. For those that are partially retail related, estimates will be needed for the portion that is related to retail.

Classification

Until this point, the discussion has described the NAICS classification of businesses in the abstract. However, the classification scheme needs to be applied to a specific set of businesses using a set procedure to determine the classification for each business unit. See Box 3-3 for a brief introduction to guidelines for classification.

Each statistical agency independently uses NAICS guidelines to classify establishments into industries on the basis of their primary activity, as measured in that agency's data, and updates that classification on its own agency schedule. Generally, for an establishment engaging in more than one activity, the entire employment of the establishment is included under the industry indicated by the primary activity.[5] Because business registers rely on different underlying source data, the Census Bureau and BLS may assign the same establishment to different industries or record the establishment with a different employment level.

There is even less agreement concerning the assignment of a code to *enterprises*, because such classification is not required under NAICS. In fact, BLS does not assign NAICS codes to enterprises. Some agencies choose to assign NAICS codes to enterprises based on their own internal data, and

---

[5]Some large companies report different activities at the same location as separate profit centers. The Census Bureau's County Business Patterns and Statistics of US Businesses (SUSB) program treats each profit center as a separate establishment. The Economic Census reporting may combine the profit centers into one establishment. This results in establishment count differences due to differences in how the data are collected. See https://www.census.gov/programs-surveys/cbp/technical-documentation/methodology.html#par_textimage_36648475.

BOX 3-3
NAICS Classification and Designation of Auxiliaries

The NAICS classification is based on a production-oriented or supply-based conceptual framework. It groups and classifies establishments according to similarities in the processes they use to produce goods or services. NAICS makes no distinction between auxiliary and operating establishments, and it recognizes the unique nature of corporate, subsidiary, and regional managing offices by including an industry code for Corporate, Subsidiary, and Regional Managing Offices (NAICS 551114, classified under sector 55).

Under NAICS, an establishment is classified under an industry when its primary activity meets the definition of that industry. Because establishments may perform more than one activity, there are procedures for identifying the primary activity of an establishment. Ideally, the principal product or service should be determined by its relative share of current production costs and capital investment. In practice, however, it is often necessary to use other variables, such as revenue, shipments, or employment as proxies for measuring significance. The most commonly used proxy measure for production in determining primary activity has been receipts or sales.

A NAICS industry may include both establishments that produce output for sale to others (market transactions) and establishments that produce output for other establishments of the same company (support activities) without a fee. Some establishments may be engaged in both support and market activities, and when this is the case their classification is based on the establishment's primary activity. Receipts reported by establishments on surveys are for their market activity and exclude the contribution of support activities; nevertheless, receipts for such secondary activities are becoming more prevalent as support facilities attempt to maximize capacity utilization.

Support activity is considered a primary activity only when it takes place in a separate establishment of a multi-establishment firm where the market activity (if any) is secondary or unrelated to the primary objective of the enterprise. Such establishments, where support is a primary activity, are designated auxiliaries if they are classified in one of six industries in the services sector: NAICS 48-49 (Transportation and Warehousing), NAICS 51 (Information), NAICS 54 (Professional, Scientific and Technical), NAICS 55 (Management of Companies or Enterprises), NAICS 56 (Administration and Support and Waste Management and Remediation), and NAICS 81 (other services except public administration). Data used for classification and designation are maintained in the Census Bureau's Business Register.

SOURCE: Based on Clarification Memo no. 3, "Classifying SIC Auxiliary Establishments in NAICS." See https://www.census.gov/eos/www/naics/history/history.html.

some may ask respondents to report the code that best describes their primary business activity. The Census Bureau's Statistics of U.S. Businesses classifies enterprises in this way:

> An enterprise may have establishments in many different industries. For the purpose of classifying an entire enterprise into a single industry, the classification methodology starts by excluding nonoperating establishments—establishments classified as manufacturers' sales branches and offices, establishments engaged in management of enterprises and enterprises (NAICS 55), and auxiliary establishments. The enterprise is then classified into the 2-digit NAICS sector in which it paid the largest share of its payroll. Then, within this 2-digit NAICS sector, the enterprise is classified into the 3-digit NAICS subsector in which the enterprise paid the largest share of payroll. Finally, within the assigned 3-digit NAICS sub-sector, the enterprise is classified into the 4-digit NAICS industry group with the largest share of payroll.[6]

One of the challenges with enterprise classification is that the "primary sector" is likely to change over time as business lines evolve and establishments are bought and sold.

Ideally, the NAICS coding of establishments would be applied uniformly, with all federal statistical agencies using the same code for each business unit. However, this is effectively impossible in the U.S. context, due to laws that restrict the sharing of individually identifiable information, even across federal statistical agencies. As a result, the two agencies that provide data related to business output and employment, the Census Bureau and BLS, each develop their own address lists and classifications of business establishments, with limited ability to share and compare them.[7]

---

[6] See https://www.census.gov/programs-surveys/susb/technical-documentation/methodology.html. An enterprise may consist of groups of establishments that operate in different sectors. Each such group may be referred to as a "firm" for purposes of reporting to annual, quarterly, and monthly surveys described later in this document.

[7] As a result of the Confidential Information Protection and Statistical Efficiency Act of 2002, BLS now receives annually the list of enterprises and the Employer Identification Numbers (EINs) that are associated with them as well as business names, addresses, and industry codes from the Census Bureau's Business Register. However, the panel was told that merging the two lists is a time-consuming, resource-intensive exercise, because in many cases different EINs are recorded on the two lists. In an email from Ken Robertson on September 2, 2020, BLS observed that an enterprise can and often does have multiple EINs. Consider a large enterprise with 60 subcomponents. The company might register one EIN with IRS for the entire enterprise, or it might register one EIN for each subcomponent. It might report 20 of those 60 EINs to the Census Bureau, aggregating 3 subcomponents each into each of 20 reports, and list a different 20 when reporting on employment to BLS, or report all 60 to one agency but not the other. Even within the Census Bureau, an enterprise may use one EIN to report payroll and another to report revenue. So, even with Census and BEA data we have incom-

Business Registers

A long-standing issue for the U.S. federal statistical system has been the fact that the economic and business surveys conducted by the Census Bureau and those conducted by BLS rely on samples drawn from separate business registers (sampling frames), with different strengths and weaknesses (Fairman et al., 2008; Fixler and Landefeld, 2006). More recent updates are described in National Academies of Sciences, Engineering, and Medicine ([NASEM], 2017, p. 41):

> The Census Bureau is able to access federal tax information from the IRS for a specified set of purposes (Internal Revenue Code 6103(j)) . . . [The] Census Bureau uses those data to create the Census Business Register; however, BLS does not currently have access to those data and so has to base its frame on a different source. Because BLS and the Census Bureau both conduct different surveys of businesses using different frames, there have been long-standing issues in comparing and reconciling the different statistics that describe the economy from the two agencies (National Research Council, 2007). The Bureau of Economic Analysis (BEA) has acknowledged the differences and cannot resolve them. Being able to use the same business list and synchronize the existing lists would both reduce the burden on businesses and improve the quality of economic statistics, and it is likely that it would also result in cost savings (National Research Council, 2007). The situation is particularly frustrating since BLS and the Census Bureau have had explicit legal authority to allow them to share business information for statistical purposes since 2002 (PL 107-347 Title V, Subtitle B). The required change to the IRS legislation that would permit BLS to have access to limited business tax information has not been passed, despite numerous efforts.[8]

More recently, in November 2020, the American Economic Association provided a letter to the incoming Biden-Harris transition team regarding "Necessary Improvement in the U.S. Statistical Infrastructure."[9] Under the seventh bullet in that letter, the association makes these points:

---

plete information about enterprises. An article that BLS has published profiling these data is available at https://www.bls.gov/opub/mlr/2016/article/establishment-firm-or-enterprise.htm.

[8]The Obama administration pushed for this legislative authority (see, e.g., U.S. Department of the Treasury, 2014; U.S. Office of Management and Budget, 2016), but despite support from previous administrations and broad support from the statistical and research community no action has been taken for this limited data sharing of business tax information for exclusively statistical purposes by Census, BEA, and BLS (see http://www.copafs.org/UserFiles/fle/FederalBusinessRegistryLetterSenatewithAttach.pdf).

[9]See https://www.aeaweb.org/content/file?id=13507.

MEASURING RETAIL EMPLOYMENT AND LABOR PRODUCTIVITY

The Executive Branch and the Congress need to resolve critical problems resulting from the decentralized nature of the Federal Statistical System, which confounds accuracy and consistency. For example: The Treasury Department must support, and the Congress must revise, Title 26, the Internal Revenue Code, to codify data sharing among BEA, Census, and BLS as routine practice. The consequential reconciliation of currently differing BLS and Census Bureau business registers will substantially improve the accuracy and comparability of major economic statistics used for business and public policy decision-making.

As described in the National Academies' report (NASEM, 2017, p. 41), "the Census Bureau's Business Register is a listing of all legal business entities—incorporated businesses, partnerships, and sole proprietorships—operating in the United States and its territories (island areas) as identified by the U.S. Internal Revenue Service (IRS). It lists businesses that have paid employees (i.e., employer businesses), of which about 5 million have only one location and 160,000 have more than one location. It also lists nonemployer businesses, of which there are about 25 million."

The National Academies' report (NASEM, 2017, pp. 42, 43) goes on to say that

> this Business Register combines data from multiple sources with the goal of providing comprehensive, accurate, and timely coverage of business units. Administrative records are the foundation of the Business Register. The primary data for identifying businesses come from the IRS, which provides information from its Business Master File, income tax returns, and quarterly payroll tax returns. The IRS provides updates to the Census Bureau for each of these types of records on a weekly basis. The Business Master File records are a source of information on name, address, and legal form of organization for all of the Employer Identification Number (EIN) entities of which the IRS is aware. Tax records provide information on revenues, assets, inventories, payroll, employment, and industry. EIN applications filed with the IRS and processed by the Social Security Administration are shared with the Census Bureau on a monthly basis and provide NAICS codes for new businesses.[10]

The Business Register is updated with information from the IRS, the Economic Censuses, the Company Organization Survey (see Box 3-8), the Census Bureau's Business and Professional Classification Survey, and the Annual Survey of Manufacturers (but no other annual economic surveys).

The Business Register for BLS is designed to support BLS's Quarterly Census of Employment and Wages. Establishments are classified into industries on the basis of their primary activity. For an establishment engaging

---

[10] BLS does not have access to IRS data.

in more than one activity, the entire employment of the establishment is included under the industry indicated by the principal activity. Industry information is also collected on a supplement to the quarterly unemployment insurance tax reports filed by employers.

The Quarterly Census of Employment and Wages, which consists of a monthly count of employment and quarterly counts of wage levels and business establishments, covers greater than 95 percent of the jobs available in the United States. The primary source for this census is administrative data from state unemployment insurance programs. These data are supplemented by data from two BLS surveys: the Annual Refiling Survey and the Multiple Worksite Report.

As reported by the National Academies (NASEM, 2017, p. 43),

> each quarter, the Census Bureau prepares a listing of unclassified or partially classified EINs to refer to the BLS for comparison with its Business Register. The BLS provides approximately 30 percent of industry codes for EINs that appear on the Census Bureau's list, mostly for small employers. In addition to providing data that would otherwise be missing, this operation helps to make the Census Bureau's Business Register more consistent with the separate BLS register.

In 2004, BLS and the Census Bureau reinitiated a project to compare and contrast the two registers. Preliminary results, reported by Becker and colleagues (2005), used an aggregate analysis comparing 2001 data from the Census Bureau's *County Business Patterns* to data from BLS's *Quarterly Census of Employment and Wages*. They observe that there are four main types of known differences between the two lists: differences in collection (the surveys used to maintain the lists), differences in scope (the parts of the economy covered by the data), data definitions (e.g., agencies use different definitions—for payroll and for designation of a company as "active"), and differences in reference period. If adjustments are made for these known differences, establishment counts and wages at the national level are similar, but employment differences remain. One of the challenges encountered in making comparisons at the sectoral level was that in 2001, BLS data were classified based on 2002 NAICS codes, while Census data were classified based on 1997 NAICS codes. The sectors impacted most by this difference were retail trade (NAICS 44-45), wholesale trade (NAICS 42), and information (NAICS 51).

Fairman and colleagues (2008) report on the follow-on study, a microdata match between the two registers. Of the 6.1 million unique EINs in the BLS and Census registers in 2003, only about 75 percent matched. They concluded: "while it seems likely that differences in establishment classification by Census and BLS at the same companies may explain a substantial part of the industry differences between the two lists, the lack of a common establishment-level identifier makes matching individual establishments and comparing their industry codes very difficult" (pp. 5, 6).

One of the industry differentials they observed was an apparent misclassification of the headquarters operations for mining companies in Texas. These tended to be assigned by BLS to the category of Mining and by Census to Management (a category that includes auxiliaries). The paper concluded that "it is difficult to determine the best way to classify these establishments" (Fairman et al., 2008, p. 4). In general, BLS has limited information as a basis for designating auxiliaries.

Impact of Differences

Even when the concepts being measured are the same, some differences will emerge in the estimates by the two agencies due to their separate sources of data, separate processes for maintaining business registers, and the fact that different classifications may be assigned to the same enterprise by the two agencies. See Tables 3-1a and 3-1b for a comparison of the number of establishments and the number of employees estimated to fall under different NAICS codes as measured by three programs: the Economic Census (under the Census Bureau), the Statistics of US Businesses (also under the Census Bureau), and the Quarterly Census of Employers (under BLS).

The largest percent differences are in the establishment counts, between that of the Economic Census and that of the Quarterly Census of Employers, with the latter generally having larger counts and with percent differences ranging from −2.1 to 33.3 percent. The percent differences in employment are smaller, ranging from −5.5 to 10.6 percent. These latter percentages may provide a clue as to the impact of differences in classification on the numerator (output data collected by Census) and denominator (input data collected by BLS).

> CONCLUSION 3-2: Labor productivity is measured as the ratio of change in output divided by change in input. Given that nominal output is measured by Census Bureau surveys while labor input and price deflators are measured from the Bureau of Labor Statistics' surveys, and that the two agencies use separate business registers with separate classifications of business establishments by the North American Industry Classification System code as sampling frames for surveys, estimates of productivity are bound to contain errors. The resulting differences in statistics produced by the two agencies likely contribute to this error because different establishments may contribute to the numerator and denominator. The error most likely has a time-varying component because each agency updates its business list on a different schedule.

TABLE 3-1a Comparison of the Number of Establishments by NAICS Codes, as Measured by Three Programs, 2017

NAICS	Description	Economic Census (EC)	Statistics of US Businesses (SUSB)	Quarterly Census of Employers (QCEW)	Percent Difference (SUSB – EC) / EC	Percent Difference (QCEW – EC) / EC
42	Wholesale trade	408,333	409,656	612,359	0.3%	33.3%
44-45	Retail trade	1,064,087	1,064,449	1,042,096	0.0%	−2.1%
48-49	Transportation and warehousing	237,095	237,308	242,932	0.1%	2.4%
481	Air transportation	4,450	4,441	5,784	−0.2%	23.1%
483	Water transportation	1,643	1,668	2,063	1.5%	20.4%
484	Truck transportation	126,803	126,986	127,366	0.1%	0.4%
492	Couriers and messengers	14,467	14,359	17,407	−0.7%	16.9%
493	Warehousing and storage	16,956	16,901	17,389	−0.3%	2.5%

TABLE 3-1b Comparison of the Estimated Number of Employees by NAICS Codes, as Measured by Three Programs

NAICS	Description	Economic Census (EC)	Statistics of US Businesses (SUSB)	Quarterly Census of Employers (QCEW)	Percent Difference (SUSB – EC) / EC	Percent Difference (QCEW – EC) / EC
42	Wholesale trade	6,242,335	6,115,476	5,898,637	−2.0%	−5.5%
44-45	Retail trade	15,938,821	15,705,808	15,854,454	−1.5%	−0.5%
48-49	Transportation and warehousing	4,954,931	4,866,282	4,947,369	−1.8%	−0.2%
481	Air transportation	508,300	470,353	493,349	−7.5%	−2.9%
483	Water transportation	62,745	61,762	64,276	−1.6%	2.4%
484	Truck transportation	1,480,107	1,465,040	1,452,674	−1.0%	−1.9%
492	Couriers and messengers	633,108	641,572	666,600	1.3%	5.3%
493	Warehousing and storage	921,320	913,559	1,018,613	−0.8%	10.6%

CONCLUSION 3-3: The Bureau of Labor Statistics (BLS) annually receives a file containing Census Bureau Firm IDs, Employee Identification Numbers (EINs), and establishment detail. However, BLS does not use the Census file on a regular basis because the reconciliation of EINs between Census and BLS is labor intensive and time consuming. It would be beneficial to be able to quantify all of the activity under firm IDs that have some establishments classified as retail and for which linking BLS and Census firm and establishment data might help in identifying retail-related auxiliaries in BLS data, for example, something that is not currently possible. This has the potential for helping in the development of a satellite account on activities supporting retail trade.

CONCLUSION 3-4: A study using the Census Bureau's firm-level microdata and other relevant information could be designed to develop factors to adjust for systematic differences between numerator and denominator to improve productivity estimates.

CONCLUSION 3-5: The ideal long-term solution to the issue of separate business registers being developed, maintained, and used by the Bureau of Labor Statistics and the Census Bureau would be to remove the obstacles to data sharing noted in National Academies of Sciences, Engineering, and Medicine (2017) and National Research Council (2007) and for the federal government to develop and use a single common business register.

MEASURING OUTPUT

Conceptual Issues in Measuring Nominal Output

A central part of measuring labor productivity is measuring the real output of an industry and the way it changes over time. This discussion is divided into two sections, because there are two substantial issues that need to be addressed: the concept of output that forms the basis of the measurement and the price indices that are used to deflate nominal measures of output to adjust for inflation. This section addresses the output concept and its measurement; the next section addresses the price indices.

As noted in the previous chapter and above in this chapter, output in the retail-related sector is defined in four different ways[11] in the federal

---

[11] Note that none of these output measures addresses household tastes, so they have no way of measuring the effect of increased product variety on consumer welfare, as explored by Neiman and Vavra (2019). It is not clear how the increase in product variety could be appropriately reflected in the output measure.

statistical system: (1) as total sales revenue; (2) as the difference between sales revenue and the cost of goods sold (gross margin); (3) as the difference between sales revenue and the cost of all purchased inputs (value added); and (4) as the difference between sales revenue and the cost of all inputs purchased within the sector (sectoral output). This conceptual discussion focuses on the contrasts in the first three definitions (see Box 3-4), since sectoral output varies with the definition of the sector, ranging from sales revenue (for narrow definitions of the sector) to value added (when the sector encompasses the entire economy).

BLS has said[12] that for most service industries, and in particular the retail-related service industries, sectoral output nearly equals the gross sales or revenue of the industry, because intra-industry transfers are tiny or even nonexistent. Hence, for purposes of measuring the output of retail-related industries, sectoral output is approximately equal to gross sales but is more complex to compute. Hence, gross sales provides a reasonable simple approximation to nominal output for the service industries. However, the observation that intra-industry transfers are tiny for the service industries may be a reflection of data gaps.

Conceptually, a sales revenue measure of retail output uses the retail sales price of a product as the measure. That price reflects the entire chain of processes that goes into the product, from its initial design to the raw materials to the manufacture to the multiple steps involved in providing the product for sale and delivering it to the final customer. In other words, it includes the contributions of the entire value chain in the production and distribution of the good, not just the value added by the retailer. In contrast, a value-added measure of retail output focuses on the portion of the product's value directly provided by the retailer, subtracting the wholesale cost of the product and any other purchased inputs that the retailer does not provide. Thus, the value-added measure of output directly isolates the portion of the value chain that is produced by the retail firm's own labor and capital. Between these two concepts, the gross margin measure removes the wholesale cost of the product, which reflects the value related to its design and manufacture, but includes the value added by other factors besides the retailer's own labor and capital, such as the value provided by leasing a store or paid to another vendor who handles customer service.

Strictly speaking, the value-added measure of output is the one that is associated with the services provided by the retailer that derive from the

---

[12]Email from Jenny Rudd, BLS October 21, 2020: "In most cases the sectoral output of a service industry nearly equals the gross output of the industry. Because intra-industry transfers are tiny or even non-existent, the values for the two output concepts overlap. We have looked into the possibility of adding intra-industry adjustments to service industries. The problem is that the data to do so from the input-output (IO) tables are generally not at a detailed enough level."

> **BOX 3-4**
> **Alternative Measures of Nominal Output**
>
> *Gross sales* are often used as a measure of gross output for retail-related services.
>
> *Gross margins*, or as they are also called, trade and transport margins, are used by the U.S. National Accounts, and by the international handbook, the *System of National Accounts*, as the appropriate measure of the gross output of the trade and transport industries (wholesale, retail, and transportation of goods). Unlike other industries, these trade industries do not transform goods from intermediate materials into finished goods. Rather, they buy finished goods for resale, with little or no transformation of the product. Hence, for these industries output is best measured by the services they provide—including advertising, information and display of products, inventorying, and delivery—which can be measured by their sales less their cost of goods sold.
>
> *Value-added estimates* exclude all inputs purchased by the industry and are therefore the only output measure that does not double count some outputs across industries. As a result, the sum of value-added by industry equals GDP. Gross margins, while useful, are not a pure measure of trade industry output or productivity, because like gross sales for other industries, they still contain double counting for other intermediate inputs, like energy and purchased services. The appropriate measure of the unduplicated output of any industry is value added, measured as gross sales less all intermediate inputs (or the sum of labor compensation, profits, proprietor's income, and rents and other capital income).

capital used and the activities of the retailer's employees who provide the labor input used to calculate labor productivity. Of particular importance, the value-added measure of output is the only measure that makes the adjustments necessary to compare the labor productivities of large national retail chains and small mom-and-pop stores on an equal footing, in each case removing the contributions to total sales revenue that are provided by the workers at other firms. However, not all analysts are persuaded that the value-added measure is superior; some analysts are concerned that a value-added measure of output can be distorted by monopoly pricing (e.g., Walter Oi, cited by Manser, 2005). In fact, all three measures are potentially influenced by varying markups. Value-added measures are in a sense residual measures, reflecting the effect of business cycles, shifts in demand, and input cost changes, and this can make them quite volatile.

Despite the conceptual differences across these three output measures, they are clearly related, and under some conditions they will produce similar measures of labor productivity change. Specifically, in cases where the contributions of the different inputs are fixed, the three output measures will move proportionally. For example, if the cost of the goods represents one-third of the sales price, and the cost of the store lease and other purchased services represents one-third of the sales price, then the gross margin will be two-thirds of total sales revenue and value-added will be one-third of total sales revenue. In this simple fixed case, the three different output measures will all increase by the same percentage. As a result, if the industry is relatively stable, all three measures will show roughly the same change.

However, if the industry is experiencing change, with different parts of the value chain growing more or less quickly than others, then the three different output measures are likely to show different percentage changes. It would be reasonable to expect the retail sector to show such differences at this time, given the kinds of transformation discussed in the previous chapter. And indeed, Figure 2-1 in that chapter shows that the three different measures of retail output produce three different estimates of labor productivity growth for the 1997-2018 period. That implies three different estimates of output growth, since all three estimates use the same measure of the change in labor input. Figure 2-1 also shows that sales revenue for the retail sector overall grew faster than gross margin, which in turn grew faster than value-added. Given the relationships between these measures, these inequalities imply that the cost of goods sold grew faster than the gross margin, and that the contribution of other purchased factors grew faster than the value added by retailers' own labor and capital. These different growth rates in the other sectors related to retail—particularly those that produce other services purchased by retail firms—provide some hints of the restructuring occurring.[13]

> CONCLUSION 3-6: The nominal output of the retail and related sectors is measured in several different ways in the federal statistical system. A sales revenue measure of output is the simplest to produce but does not reflect changes in a retailer's cost structure when additional functions—like warehousing—are integrated into the business. It does not focus on the services the retail sector provides, either. A value-added measure of output is theoretically preferred for measuring labor productivity in retail, capturing the difference between gross output and intermediate inputs, but there are limits in the ability to obtain the data needed to produce value-added measures. A gross margin measure of output reflects the value of the most important input for a retailer—the cost of goods sold—while sidestepping problems related to estimating other inputs. Because the extra data on purchases and

---

[13] This paragraph slightly oversimplifies the comparison, since the labor productivity comparisons in Figure 2-1 show changes in real—not nominal—labor productivity, so differences in both nominal output measures and price deflation will affect the comparison.

other inputs are not published for as many detailed North American Industry Classification System codes as for sales, gross margin and value-added measures are available for fewer detailed retail industries. For retail-supporting services that might be combined with retail trade in a broader retail-related sector, similar choices would need to be made concerning which measure of nominal output to use, and those choices would entail tradeoffs between simplicity of data and conceptual focus. When the retail sector experiences significant change, the different output measures will give different pictures of labor productivity growth, depending on the extent to which the change is occurring for the retail services themselves, the various retail-supporting services provided by other suppliers, or the products provided for sale.

Federal Data and Issues for Measuring Output

The following sections discuss the statistical programs of the U.S. Census Bureau that collect retail-related data for measuring output (sales, revenue, or value of shipments; purchases; detailed expenses; and transfers between establishments) including the Annual, Quarterly, and Monthly Economic Surveys, the Economic Census, and other every-5-year collections.

The Census Bureau, like other statistical agencies, collects information in a time sequence ranging from simple statistics published frequently to more detailed statistics published with longer delays. The quality of the early estimates is lower, because samples are smaller and respondent-provided data may consist of estimates made by businesses. There is typically more detail provided with later estimates, because they have larger sample sizes, and there is more time to clean the data. This time sequence and the use of benchmarking mean that there may be very long delays before final data are available. For example, the detailed data from the Annual Retail Trade Survey (ARTS) for 2018 were released in February 2020 and were benchmarked to the 2012 Economic Census (because 2017 Economic Census data were not yet available.)

The Census Bureau's Monthly, Quarterly, and Annual Economic Surveys

The Monthly Retail Trade Survey and Advance Monthly Retail Trade Survey collect sales data from a sample of retail firms[14] that report for their retail establishments. Data from the former are published within 50 days of the close of the reference month, while data from the latter are published

---

[14]We use the term "firm" to distinguish a group of establishments within an enterprise, all of which are either classified in (say) retail trade or classified as supporting establishments for retail trade. An enterprise may contain many such firms.

within 20 days. Both surveys provide estimates with less NAICS detail than ARTS provides.

The Monthly Wholesale Trade Survey collects data from a sample of U.S. merchant wholesalers (excluding manufacturers' sales branches and offices) on monthly sales, end-of-month inventories, and number of enterprises reported for. Data are released about 40 days after the close of the reference month and are provided with less NAICS detail than for the Annual Wholesale Trade Survey (AWTS).

The Quarterly Services Survey collects total sales, receipts, revenue, and total operating expenses from a sample of firms with establishments in selected services industries. Estimates are released about 50 days after the close of the reference quarter, and the data are provided with less NAICS detail than for the Services Annual Survey (SAS).

The surveys summarized in Box 3-5 collect economic detail for retail and retail-related industries in the three annual surveys mentioned above: ARTS (retail), AWTS (wholesale), and SAS (services). ARTS provides data on nominal gross sales, purchases, and gross margins for establishments classified in the retail sector. AWTS provides nominal gross sales, operating expenses, gross margins, and purchases for establishments classified in the wholesale sector.[15] And SAS provides revenue and total expenses for establishments classified in the services sector, which includes transportation and warehousing. Except as noted, for all three surveys data are provided at the 4-digit NAICS level, with some 5- and 6-digit detail. The exceptions are that ARTS provides estimates of purchases, gross margins, and total expenses only at the 3-digit NAICS level, with some 4- and 5-digit NAICS level detail; for transportation industries in SAS, 3-digit NAICS level data are also provided for detailed expenses and commodity-level revenue.

For the margin industries (retail and wholesale), there is a data gap in integrating the Economic Census data with the annual surveys. In the annual surveys, gross margins are measured at the industry level of detail (mostly 3-digit). In the Economic Census data, gross revenue is collected at a detailed product-group level, but no information is collected on gross margins. This implies that gross margins at the product-group level are never directly measured but only inferred by combining this disparate

---

[15]To create the sampling frame for the Monthly Retail Trade Survey and ARTS (same approach used for the Monthly Wholesale Trade Survey and AWTS) all employer establishments located in the United States and classified in the retail trade and accommodation and foot-services sectors are sorted by EINs or firm identifiers. The establishment data for the EIN/firm (potentially only part of an enterprise) are aggregated to become potential sampling units. The sample is selected by a stratified design and selected firms/EINs are asked to report for the aggregate of their retail establishments and retail auxiliaries. Thus, the survey data statistically represent retail establishments. See https://www.census.gov/retail/mrts/how_surveys_are_collected.html.

BOX 3-5
The Census Bureau's Annual Economic Surveys

Annual Retail Trade Survey (ARTS) (NAICS 44, 45)
  Representation: Retail trade establishments in the United States; no establishment detail collected.
  When released: About 15 months after close of reference year.
  Variables: Sales, e-commerce sales, end-of-year inventories, purchases, gross margins, and total operating expenses.
  Level of detail: Sales and operating expenses are reported at the sector, subsector, and industry levels, with some 5- and 6-digit detail. End-of-year inventories, purchases, and gross margins are reported at the sector and subsector levels with some 4- and 5-digit detail. E-commerce sales are reported at the sector and subsector levels and one 4-digit industry detail.

Annual Wholesale Trade Survey (AWTS) (NAICS 42)
  Representation: Wholesale trade establishments in the United States; no establishment detail collected.
  When released: About 14 months after close of reference year.
  Variables: Sales, e-commerce sales, end-of-year inventories, purchases, gross margins, total operating expenses, and commissions.
  Level of detail: Sales, purchases, gross margins, e-commerce sales, end-of-year-inventories, and operating expenses are reported at the sector, subsector, and industry levels, with some 5-digit detail. Commissions are reported at the industry level for electronic markets, agents, and brokers.

Services Annual Survey (SAS) (NAICS 22, 48-49, 51, 52, 53, 54, 56, 61, 62, 71, 72, and 81)
  Representation: Service industry establishments in the United States; no establishment detail collected. Of special interest to the study of retail-related industries are warehousing and transportation (48, 49).
  When released: No later than 13 months after close of reference year.
  Variables: Revenue, sources of revenue, total and detailed operating expenses by product.
  Level of detail: Total revenue and total expenses are reported at the 2-, 3-, and 4-digit NAICS code levels, with some 5- and 6-code detail. For NAICS 48 and 49, detailed operating expenses are published for most 2- and 3-digit NAICS codes (for transportation this includes Purchased Freight Transportation), sources of revenue are provided for a number of transportation categories, and revenue sources by commodity handled are provided for Truck Transportation (484).

information measured at different frequencies. This is a potential source of measurement error, including mismatches between the price deflators at the product-group level and the measured nominal gross margins.

The sampling units for ARTS, AWTS, and SAS are enterprises that are asked to report for the aggregates of their retail, wholesale, or services establishments (respectively) plus the auxiliaries that support those industries. The only exception is that enterprises reporting on ARTS are asked to exclude auxiliaries from their retail sales aggregates. The enterprises are asked to break out the industry detail if, for example, an enterprise with retail activity has establishments in multiple retail industries. If enterprises do not provide this detail, their allocation to an industry category is based on administrative data and the Economic Censuses.

The Census Bureau's Economic Census and Related Surveys

As illustrated in Box 3-6, the Economic Census provides measures of gross sales, payroll, first quarter payroll, and number of employees every 5 years. Data are collected at the establishment level and are available at the U.S. level with 6-digit NAICS code detail as well as at the product code level (the Business Expense Supplement to ARTS and AWTS provides detailed expense data at the enterprise level every 5 years). The Commodity Flow Survey, sponsored by the Bureau of Transportation Statistics and collected by the Census Bureau, is also conducted every 5 years to describe domestic freight shipments by establishments in the mining, manufacturing, wholesale, auxiliaries, and selected retail and services trade industries located in the 50 states and the District of Columbia. The Commodity Flow Survey is of potential importance to this project because data reported on a transported commodity may indicate whether the shipment is for retail (e.g., TVs or clothing) or wholesale (e.g., jet engines or elevator assemblies).

Differences in the unit of observation and the range of data collected in ARTS, relative to that collected in the Census for Retail Trade (CRT), create limitations in estimating gross margins at detailed industry levels at an annual frequency. The data in ARTS are collected at the enterprise level, which limits the level of detail directly available from the survey data (although the Census Bureau requests large multi-units in multiple industries within retail to break out industry detail). Given these limitations, the data released from ARTS combines information directly from the survey data with adjustments from the Economic Census.[16] This is an imperfect process in a number of ways. For example, the release of the 2018 Annual Retail Trade data in February 2020 uses adjustments from the 2012 Economic Census, because the 2017 Economic Census tabulations were not yet

---

[16] See https://www.census.gov/data/tables/2018/econ/arts/annual-report.html.

**BOX 3-6
The Census Bureau's 5-Year Surveys
(conducted in years ending in "2" and "7")**

Economic Census
Representation: Establishments covering most industries and all geographic areas of the United States.
When released: First release typically 18-24 months after the close of the reference year.
Key variables: Number of firms, number of establishments, sales, annual payroll, first quarter payroll, and number of employees. These are provided for most industries, including retail (NAICS 44-45), wholesale (NAICS 42), and transportation and warehousing (NAICS 48-49). Wholesale trade tables also include total operating expenses.
Level of detail: At the U.S. level, tables provide six-digit NAICS code detail and select 7- and 8-digit details.

Business Expense Supplement (questions added to ARTS and AWTS during economic census years)
Representation: Establishments in retail and wholesale trade industries in the United States. No establishment detail collected.
When released: About 15 months after close of reference year with ARTS data and about 14 months after close of reference year with AWTS data.
Key variables: Detailed operating expenses.
Level of detail: Reported at about the same level of detail as purchases and gross margins for ARTS. Reported at the sector, subsector, and industry levels, with some 5-digit detail for AWTS.

Commodity Flow Survey (sponsored by the Bureau of Transportation Statistics and conducted by the U.S. Census Bureau)
Representation: Establishments engaged in domestic freight shipping.
When released: 2017 data tables first released July 2020.
Key variables: Type of commodity shipped, origin, destination, value, weight, mode of transportation, distance shipped, and ton/miles.
Level of detail: Data provided for 48 industry groups, including 18 in wholesale, 2 in retail, and 1 in services. Some detail is also offered for auxiliaries that are also shippers.

---

available for these tabulations.[17] In addition, while ARTS collects information on gross margins, the Census for Retail Trade does not, which makes combining information from that census and ARTS more complicated. A

---

[17] This discussion is related to the construction of the input-output accounts by BEA. The 2012 Economic Census is the most recent Economic Census data in the BEA input-output accounts used to produce 2020 statistics on economic activity.

related problem is the computation of margin prices from the PPI to match the gross margin measure of output by industry. The changing product mix within different types of retailers is captured only once every 5 years via the Census for Retail Trade. Margin prices on different products and by outlet type vary, but the changing product mix and outlet type are not well captured in the annual, quarterly, and monthly surveys of retail trade activity.

Auxiliaries

The Economic Census collects information on auxiliaries, also called enterprise support establishments, for six industries in the services sector: NAICS 48-49 (Transportation and Warehousing), NAICS 51 (Information), NAICS 54 (Professional, Scientific and Technical), NAICS 55 (Management of Companies or Enterprises), NAICS 56 (Administration and Support and Waste Management and Remediation), and NAICS 81 (other services except public administration). Information about auxiliaries in these six industries was collected in 2012 and 2017. Included are data by 3-digit sector served, number of establishments, number of employees, payroll, and external sales or revenue receipts. In the Economic Census an auxiliary is tabulated in two places: under its own establishment NAICS code and in the tabulation of auxiliaries.[18]

The Economic Census auxiliary questionnaire is sent to establishments that are marked as auxiliaries in the Business Register. New auxiliaries are so designated based on analyst research and other information. The questionnaire obtains information for each auxiliary establishment about the main industry that it serves, classified according to 3-digit NAICS code. Using this classification, Fort and Klimek (2018) determined that 20 percent of the payroll related to the retail industry in 1997 was represented by employment in nonretail auxiliary establishments that primarily served the retail sector.[19] Most of this auxiliary payroll—15 percentage points—relates to management (NAICS 551114). The other significant industries represented in auxiliaries are Warehousing and Storage (NAICS 493, 2% of payroll), Truck Transportation (NAICS 484, 1%), Accounting Services (NAICS 5412, 1%), and Unclassified (1%).

BEA includes the Census Bureau's information about auxiliaries in its national accounts and other products. Because an auxiliary serves its

---

[18] Information on Census Bureau data on auxiliaries provided by Edward Watkins at the workshop.

[19] When calculated using employment rather than payroll, the auxiliary portion represents only 7 percent of employment related to the retail industry in 1997. This auxiliary portion of employment is substantially lower than the auxiliary portion of payroll because employees in the establishments related to firm management are compensated at a higher rate than those in many other establishments.

enterprise, it does not report output data related to its support functions on the census. Any profits or earnings that accrue because of the contribution of auxiliaries to their enterprise are not captured in current data. BEA measures the service outputs of auxiliaries using data on expenses.[20]

Table 3-2 shows the Census 2012 data on auxiliaries in the six sectors that report that they serve the retail trade (by 3-digit NAICS code). The table shows that in 2012, 73 percent of the auxiliaries serving retail trade were in Administration and Support and Waste Management and Remediation, and 23 percent were in Transportation.

Those auxiliaries reporting that they serve a retail firm seem to be exactly the type of establishments that should be included in a retail-related satellite account, regardless of where they are classified. However, data on auxiliaries or support establishments are currently collected and available through the Economic Census only for establishments classified in six industries. Other information about such service establishments may be available in the microdata available at the Census Bureau.

The panel proposes that a study should be undertaken, using the Census Bureau's microdata[21] that include firm IDs as well as establishment data, to gain insights into how enterprises are structured and how support establishments might be identified. One could imagine a new public domain data product that uses this information to quantify support services. Additionally, the study could inform further work on improving the collection of data on auxiliaries and possibly improving information to estimate the value they provide to their enterprises.

CONCLUSION 3-7: Data available from the Economic Census and the Economic Surveys for the retail trade-related industries limit the ability to estimate output for retail-related industries in important ways:

- Purchase data are needed to compute gross margins, but the only purchase data for retail are collected on the Annual Retail Trade Survey (ARTS), not the Economic Census. As a result, purchase data are not available at the establishment level for retail establishments, so benchmarking to the Economic Census requires assumptions that likely affect the quality of estimated gross margins.
- ARTS does not have the same product detail for sales as in the retail trade component of the Economic Census, and it does not request any industry breakdown of activity. However, such detailed data are needed to accurately and separately allocate

---

[20]Reported by Jon Samuels during the workshop.
[21]Through a Federal Statistical Research Data Center.

TABLE 3-2 Number of Auxiliary Establishments That Supported Retail Trade, 2012 Economic Census

NAICS Served	Title	NAICS Code of Auxiliary									
		48 # Est	51 # Est	54 # Est	55 # Est	56 # Est	81 # Est
44-45	Retail trade	3,296	53	224	10,222	238	316
441	Motor vehicle and parts dealers	197	0	8	492	6	16
442	Furniture and home furnishings stores	506	2	49	357	7	5
443	Electronics and appliance stores	92	17	10	407	41	19
444	Building material, garden equipment and supplies dealers	191	3	7	460	13	4
445	Food and beverage stores	710	4	10	950	6	4
446	Health and personal care stores	129	3	5	966	12	2
447	Gasoline stations	65	11	7	845	4	6
448	Clothing and clothing accessories stores	254	3	40	1,717	9	161
451	Sporting goods, hobby, book, and music stores	111	0	1	553	8	6
452	General merchandise stores	594	8	43	2,447	30	80
453	Miscellaneous store retailers	266	1	25	579	72	5
454	Nonstore retailers	181	1	19	449	30	8
	Percentage of total	23.0	0.4	1.6	71.2	1.7	2.2

NOTES: Data on auxiliaries in 2017 Economic Census not available until September 2021.

sales and purchases to codes; their absence may affect the quality of estimated gross margins.
- Data on operating expenses are needed to compute value added. Operating expenses for retail and wholesale trade establishments are collected as an aggregate of an enterprise's establishments on ARTS[22] and Annual Wholesale Trade Survey once every 5 years during Economic Census years. Data on expenses are not collected at the establishment level in the Economic Census.
- Auxiliaries are a key concept for quantifying the impact of vertical integration in a retail-related satellite account. Though some data are available from the Economic Census, there are limited ways to estimate the value an auxiliary establishment provides to its enterprise, and the Bureau of Labor Statistics currently has limited information to designate auxiliaries that support retail.

ADJUSTING NOMINAL OUTPUT FOR CHANGES IN PRICES

After obtaining a measure of the nominal output of the retail sector, that estimate must be adjusted to remove the effect of price changes to identify the real changes in the output of the sector. This step is crucial for determining productivity, because nominal output figures can be strongly affected by inflation or deflation, particularly in a sector undergoing rapid change.

The price adjustment required will depend on the type of nominal output measure used: a sales revenue measure of retail output is deflated using the CPI. A gross margin measure of retail output is deflated using the PPI for the retail margin. A value-added measure of retail output is deflated by using the PPI for the retail margin component and other PPI indices for the other inputs. Similarly, the price adjustment for the various retail-supporting industries, such as warehousing and transportation, uses the PPI indices for those industries for a gross output measure and the analogous PPI indices for the key inputs for a value-added output measure.

This section addresses both quality adjustment, which is implemented in current U.S. price indices, and the problem of outlet substitution bias, which has been discussed in the research literature but is not reflected in U.S. economic statistics. It then provides a brief overview of the CPI and PPI indices.[23]

---

[22]See https://www.census.gov/programs-surveys/economic-census/data/bes.html.
[23]This section draws on workshop presentations by Ana Aizcorbe on the conceptual issues related to retail price indices, Brendan Williams on the CPI, and Bonnie Murphy on the PPI.

Quality Adjustment in Price Indices

Adjusting for quality is a key issue in developing price indices because potential quality differences across similar products or services make it difficult to know whether a price difference reflects a difference in the price level (indicating inflation) or a difference in quality. In the context of retail trade, "quality" refers specifically to the quality of the retail services themselves—not the quality of the products sold by retailers—and relates to the kinds of shifts the retail sector has experienced over the past few decades. As discussed in the previous chapter, the recent changes in retail have introduced different kinds of retail outlets—including warehouse stores, e-commerce, and large retailers—that provide greater product variety and different ways of obtaining and learning about products. These changes reflect changes in the quality of the services that the sector provides, and adjusting for them is necessary to determine the real output of retail services. If a gross margin or value-added measure of output is used, the quality of retail services will be reflected in a price index for the retail margin, like the PPI. If sales revenue is used to represent retail output, the quality of retail services will be reflected as one part of a price index for the product's overall sales price, like the CPI. Both types of price index are addressed here. The CPI is discussed first—because it is currently used by BLS and provides a more concrete example of the underlying concepts—but the PPI is more directly related to quality adjustment of retail services.

The simplest way to account for potential quality differences is to try to eliminate them by focusing price comparisons on products or services that are identical. When feasible, this strategy eliminates the confounding of price and quality because quality has been fixed.

The strategy of focusing on price changes for identical products is the starting point for the price comparisons used to construct the CPI itself, which collects price information across a broad range of consumer goods. A sample of products with specific characteristics is selected at a specific retail outlet, and the prices of those sampled products are collected monthly for a 4-year period and then rotated. To the extent possible, the exact same items are sampled over the entire period. If a selected item becomes unavailable, it is replaced with a comparable item, to the extent possible.

A similar approach to control for quality is used for the price information collected for the PPI for retail, which looks at changes in the average margin price (the average difference between the sales revenue and cost of goods per product) within "comparable product lines" of "related products that are distributed under a similar set of conditions."[24] The standard

---

[24] The quotes in this paragraph come from Bonnie Murphy's presentation at the workshop describing the guidelines for the PPI for retail.

guidelines for identifying the products that will be considered together call for products that are "classified within a single product category," "displayed and/or marketed in a similar manner," and "located in the same area or department of the store." By controlling these different factors that can affect the nature of the retail services offered, the PPI for retail aims to provide margin price comparisons that essentially hold constant the quality of the retail services provided.

Of course, there are cases when it is not possible to keep quality fixed and it is necessary to explicitly adjust for quality differences when comparing prices. These problems are not new conceptually: there are well-developed techniques—specifically, hedonic price indices[25]—that derive the price differences associated with different product features related to quality.

When it is not possible to find an identical or comparable item for a sampled product, BLS generally either imputes the prices of the missing items from other available observations in the sample or uses hedonic methods to estimate the previous period price for a replacement product.[26] In two important cases—computers and motor vehicles—the price adjustment is carried out using information on wholesale component costs and markups to derive a comparable price for the now-unavailable sampled product from the price of a similar but noncomparable product that is available.

Explicit quality adjustments using hedonic price techniques are not a standard feature of the PPI program that collects average margin prices for retail, although there was a program that developed a hedonic margin price model to adjust for the quality of retail services at beer, wine, and liquor stores.[27] Over a 12-year period, the program collected data related to the retail services of individual stores, including square footage, number of checkouts, number of full-time employees, number of products carried, whether product testing was conducted, whether classes were offered, and whether local deliveries were offered. This information was used to develop a model that related changes in margin prices to these characteristics. Unfortunately, the model did not show a meaningful relationship between these indicators of the quality of retail services and the change in the margin prices. Despite this failure to use hedonic price techniques to explain retail service quality changes within individual retail outlets, hedonic techniques have significantly improved the measures of important product

---

[25] Hedonic price indices analyze price changes for changing consumer products by estimating prices associated with each product's different characteristics. The price changes for the different characteristics can then be used to estimate the overall change in price for the product while controlling for the shifting characteristics.

[26] Aghion et al. (2019) argue that using prices from available observations is likely to overstate the price of missing (discontinued) items and substantially bias the CPI.

[27] This program was described by Bonnie Murphy in her workshop presentation.

classes—such as computers (Berndt, Griliches, and Rappaport, 1995)—and they could be important in understanding the differences in the quality of retail services *across* retail outlets. However, that shift raises the challenge of estimating price indices when there are shifts in consumption across retail outlets, which is addressed in the next section.

Outlet Substitution Bias

As noted above, the techniques for estimating price indices for both retail products and services—CPI and PPI, respectively—use samples of product or margin prices for individual outlets that are combined using fixed weights across outlets. However, one important aspect of the economy is the ability of consumers to move from one supplier to another, and the dynamic nature of the retail sector suggests that this type of change is clearly important in retail. When consumers shift their purchases in this way, the resulting changes in aggregate price indices for the retail sector are particularly important to reflect. The bias introduced in the price index when this shift is ignored is known in the research literature as "outlet substitution bias" (Reinsdorf, 1993).[28]

Outlet substitution bias was originally studied in the context of the earlier wave of retail transformation involving the rise of warehouse clubs and supercenters, which was discussed in the preceding chapter. These discount stores often sell the same products as more expensive stores but at generally lower prices. The effect of these stores on price level comes from the opportunity for consumers to switch from a regular store to a discount store to buy the same products for less. The major effect on average prices comes from the "outlet substitution"—consumers moving from one retail outlet to another—and not from the smaller price changes occurring at the discount stores themselves. To the extent that e-commerce products are cheaper than their in-store counterparts, e-commerce would pose a similar outlet substitution effect on the average price level.

Outlet substitution poses a conceptual challenge for the price indices currently collected by BLS, which focuses on price changes for similar goods and services at individual retail outlets. These BLS price indices weight the price changes from different outlets by their relative share at different outlets, but the *change* in relative share across outlets caused by consumers switching from one outlet to another is not reflected in the price indices. This is true for both the CPI used for sales prices and the PPI used for retail margin prices. As a result, neither the CPI nor the PPI can describe how prices change—either for the overall product or for the margin price of the

---

[28]This section draws on the workshop presentation by Ana Aizcorbe on the conceptual issues related to retail price indices.

retail services themselves—when consumers systematically move from regular stores to discount stores or from discount stores to e-commerce, except when consumers move between outlets classified in different NAICS codes.

This problem of outlet substitution bias poses a direct conceptual challenge to understanding the labor productivity effects of the transformation in retail involving warehouse clubs, supercenters, and e-commerce. If the potential price decreases from outlet substitution are not reflected in the price indices, then the estimated price increases will be too large, which will in turn make the estimates of increases in real output too low. Since price indices fail to correct for outlet substitution, they effectively miss the important productivity effects of the recent transformation in retail.

One solution to the problem of outlet substitution bias involves the use of a different kind of price index—a "unit value index"—that specifically looks at the change in the average price of a product or service over time (Nakamura et al., 2015).[29] This price index explicitly reflects changes in the distribution of sales across different outlets, allowing it to capture the effect of consumers moving to less expensive stores. To do this, however, a unit value price index requires information about the quantity of sales of each sampled product at each outlet at each time period, in addition to information about prices.

Transaction data from retailers could be used as a way of providing information about both prices and quantities of sales. (See the discussion below about private sector data sources.) The available transaction data are incomplete, with data from aggregators such as Nielsen, IRI, NPD, Affinity, and Palantir including aggregations from both scanners and credit cards but often missing key types of outlets, such as the warehouse clubs, supercenters, and e-commerce outlets of particular interest.[30]

A new data collection effort by the PPI division of BLS is collecting more detailed margin price data directly from large wholesale trade companies that would provide transaction-level data on a monthly basis electronically.[31] If this approach proves workable, it could provide a model for expanding data collection in the retail sector in a way that is easier for large

---

[29] Another solution to the problem of outlet substitution bias would involve estimating the consumer utility related to the different services that retailers offer. This potential approach would have the benefit of also providing an analysis of the consumer benefits resulting from the increased variety offered by retailers. Techniques that have been developed to analyze the consumer utility from consumer goods (e.g., Diewert and Feenstra, 2019; Feenstra, 1994; and Redding and Weinstein, 2016) could be used to do this. The panel thanks an anonymous reviewer for pointing this out.

[30] This overview of the coverage of private data sources was provided in Ana Aizcorbe's presentation at the workshop.

[31] This new data collection effort was described in Bonnie Murphy's presentation at the workshop.

companies to provide and with additional detail for price index estimation. However, the more limited coverage of this effort—likely limited to large companies that routinely make extensive use of electronic data systems—would limit its potential use for broader price indices like the CPI and PPI, which sample from all types of outlets.

The lack of the necessary quantity of information in regular reporting raises the question of understanding the size of the bias caused by outlet substitution.[32] This in turn raises the question of quality adjustment, which was discussed in the previous section. In constructing the CPI and PPI margin price indices, quality needs to be controlled or adjusted within an individual retail outlet for the products or services sampled in that outlet. However, to construct a unit value index across retail outlets, it is necessary to control or adjust quality across products or services across the full range of retail outlets, which could raise substantial comparability problems.

The difficulties of adjusting for quality raise the pragmatic question of the extent to which the size of the bias from outlet substitution could be bounded by an approach that did not attempt to adjust for quality differences. Most studies agree that outlet substitution bias generally causes price increases to be overestimated (ILO/IMF/OECD/UNECE/Eurostat/The World Bank, 2004), although Nakamura and colleagues (2015) show that the bias can go in either direction, in principle. Moulton (2018) estimates that the outlet substitution effect caused by the introduction of warehouse clubs and supercenters in the 1990s led to an overestimate of price increases by only 0.08 percentage points per year. The effect of outlet substitution bias from the growth of nonstore retailers in recent years is likely to be much smaller (Hatzius, 2017), given their relatively small share of retail sales. In any case, it is important to remember that outlet substitution bias is a problem only during the transition itself, when market shares are changing across outlets. Of course, there is likely to be the most interest in productivity statistics for the retail sector precisely when market shares are changing across outlets.

Federal Price Deflators

BLS produces the primary price deflators that are used to estimate real output from the nominal measures of output derived from Census data.

The PPI is a family of indexes that measure the average change over time in selling prices received by domestic producers of goods and services. Most useful in measuring productivity is the set of indices that uses NAICS classifications, measuring changes in prices received for an industry's output

---

[32] This discussion of the problem of estimating the bias caused by outlet substitution was provided by Ana Aizcorbe's presentation at the workshop.

sold outside the industry (that is, its net output). The prices included in the PPI are from the first commercial transaction for many products and some services. The PPI is the primary deflator source for manufacturers' sales and branch offices' sales, for truck transportation, couriers, and messengers, and for warehousing. For retail and wholesale trade, the PPI measures average margin prices for narrow product groups, calculated as the difference between the sales price and the cost of goods sold. Calculation of the PPI first captures the changes in the average margin prices for individual outlets, and then weights those individual-outlet changes according to the share of each outlet. For the PPI retail and wholesale margins, the outlet weights are based on the margin revenue for each outlet. These outlet weights are updated every 5 years using margin revenue data from the Census Bureau.[33]

The CPI is a measure of the average change over time in the prices paid by urban consumers for a market basket of consumer goods and services. Indexes are available for major groups of consumer expenditures (food and beverages, housing, apparel, transportation, medical care, recreation, education and communications, and other goods and services), for items within each group, and for special categories, such as services. The CPI-U-RS is the primary deflator source for retail trade industry sales used by the BLS industry program to obtain its labor productivity measures. Price surveys capture the changes in price of a particular item at a particular store, and as such do not capture price changes when a new retail outlet enters, nor when a service is added to the sale. The weights used to sample outlets and choose the number of price quotes for each outlet are determined by the reported expenditure shares for each item category at each outlet. These weights are updated when the outlet sample is revised in a staggered rotation of eight sampled cohorts, each lasting 4 years with one cohort being revised every 6 months. However, any implicit shift across outlets that occurs when a sample is revised to reflect current sales is not reflected in average prices, because price changes are based on only the matched model that compares current and previous period prices of the same item at the same outlet.[34]

In addition to these BLS price deflators, annual data from BEA's National Income and Product Accounts on implicit price deflators for manufacturing and trade sales are used to deflate merchant wholesale sales. An implicit price deflator is the ratio of the current-dollar value of a series, such as gross domestic product (GDP), to its corresponding chained-dollar value, multiplied by 100.

> **CONCLUSION 3-8:** Although the existing price indices provide a way of describing price changes that occur for services and products

[33] Bonnie Murphy, BLS, personal communication, October 28, 2020.
[34] Brendan Williams, BLS, personal communication, October 27, 2020.

provided by individual retail outlets, they do not typically capture the aggregate price changes that result when consumers move from one type of retail outlet to another. For example, the price indices do not reflect the change in the price and quality of retail services as consumers move from a traditional department store to a warehouse store or to e-commerce, except when consumers move between outlets classified in different North American Industry Classification System codes.

CONCLUSION 3-9: The price deflator for retail-sector industries should relate to the change in *services* the sector provides and changes in the prices and quality of those services. This differs from price adjustment related to the products the retailer sells, which is focused on the characteristics of the goods themselves. Price deflation in the retail sector needs to consider, for example, the shifts in services in moving from a traditional department store to a warehouse store to e-commerce, which involves changes related to such things as product variety and the process for identifying and obtaining goods.

MEASURING INPUT

Compared to the difficulties involved in measuring nominal output and prices, the conceptual issues related to measuring employment are more straightforward. There are two primary factors to address, one related to the quantity of labor input and the other related to its quality. Although it is convenient to refer to "employment" as the denominator of labor productivity, the correct concept is actually *quality-adjusted hours of labor*, reflecting the fact that different workers provide different numbers of hours of work (because of differences in standard hours, overtime, and paid time off) and labor of different quality (because of varying skill levels). During periods of increasing labor quality, labor inputs that are not quality-adjusted could be understated and could lead to overstatements of changes in labor productivity. Alternatively, advanced technology, such as automation or the use of scanner technology, may substitute for more skilled workers in some components of retail trade, so that there is declining labor quality.

Obtaining hours of labor requires making adjustments to convert information on employment into hours worked. These adjustments need to reflect data related to standard hours, overtime, and paid time off, in addition to information related to part-time employees. Box 3-7 describes BLS employment data.

Adjusting for labor of differing quality could be done in a variety of ways, using different empirical approaches to account for different skill levels. In practice, however, only crude measures of skill are available across the entire labor force—primarily the proxies of education, age, and

**BOX 3-7
BLS Data on Employment and Hours
for Trade-Related Industries**

Current Employment Statistics (CES)
Representation: Monthly survey of U.S. establishments covered by Unemployment Insurance. Data are collected for the pay period that includes the 12th of the month.
When released: Generally, the third Friday following the week that includes the 12th of the month.
Key variables: Nonfarm employment series for all employees and production and nonsupervisory employees. CES also produces average weekly hours (AWH) for all employees and nonsupervisory employee hours; these are hours for which pay was received.
Level of detail: Aggregation to CES-defined major industry sectors with detail at the 3- or 4-digit NAICS code level, with some 5- and 6-digit detail.

National Compensation Survey
Representation: Private industry and state and local government workers in U.S. establishments with nonfarm payrolls covered by Unemployment Insurance. Data are collected for the pay period that includes the 12th day of the month for the reference periods of March, June, September, and December.
When released: At the end of the month following the reference month.
Key variables: Hours worked (excludes leave, etc.); hours paid.
Level of detail: 3-digit industry level.

Current Population Survey
Representation: Monthly survey of U.S. households. Data are usually collected for the week that includes the 12th of the month.
When released: Generally, the third Friday following the week that includes the 12th of the month.
Key variables: Employment and hours worked for supervisors, nonsupervisors, the self-employed, and unpaid family workers.
Level of detail: A Census-defined industry coding system with 270 categories that maps to NAICS codes or aggregates of NAICS codes.

Computing Key Employment Variables from Survey Data
Hours worked for nonsupervisory payroll employees (total annual) = nonsupervisory AWH paid (CES) x [hours worked/hours paid ratio (NCS)] x nonsupervisory employment (CES) x 52 weeks.
Hours worked for supervisory payroll employees (total annual) = nonsupervisory AWH paid (CES) x [supervisor/nonsupervisory hours worked ratio (CPS)] x [hours worked/hours paid ratio (NCS)] x supervisory employment (CES) x 52 weeks.
Total hours worked = hours worked for payroll (nonsupervisory + supervisory) employees + hours worked self-employed (CPS) + hours worked unpaid family workers (CPS).

compensation.[35] As noted above, BLS measures labor quality for the multifactor productivity program using data on average wage rates for different groups of workers defined by differences in educational attainment, age, and gender. The shift in the labor force distribution across these different categories, resulting in a shift in the weighted average wage rate across the labor force, is then used to adjust the number of hours worked by the change in quality.

One challenge in implementing a broader retail satellite account is likely to be in allocating employment (or hours worked) into retail-related and nonretail-related for some NAICS codes. It is likely that this will require new data.

A final issue regarding the measurement of employment concerns properly accounting for outsourcing, that is, an establishment's use of workers from temporary agencies or a professional employer organization that has its own NAICS code. Professional employer organizations are under NAICS 56–Administrative and Support—one of the codes related to auxiliary establishments. Outsourcing makes it difficult to link the workforce to the sector in which the work is being done. Outsourcing has become common for some firms. For example, there are some Walmart distribution centers that are in-house warehouses with all workers outsourced. Although some data are available through the Census Bureau, this is another potential data gap that will require investigation.

Federal Data and Issues

Employment Statistics

The primary federal statistics for input (employment or hours worked) are collected by the BLS on an establishment basis through its Current Employment Statistics Survey and the National Compensation Survey (see Box 3-7). The Census Bureau collects data on employment and payroll (not hours worked) by establishment through its annual Company Organization Survey (see Box 3-8) and through the Economic Census.

> **CONCLUSION 3-10:** While hours worked is considered to be the appropriate measure of input for measuring labor productivity, it is improved when work hours are adjusted to reflect the quality of work provided by workers with different skill sets. Current Bureau of Labor Statistics' approaches adjust for worker quality by looking at pay

---

[35] New research by Acemoglu and Autor (2011), Autor (2013), and Acemoglu and Restrepo (2018) suggests that task-based measures of job-specific skill may be more useful measures of labor quality, which would require additional data sources.

> **BOX 3-8**
> **Census Bureau's Other Important Annual Survey**
> **(data not directly published)**
>
> **Company Organization Survey**
> *Representation*: Multi-establishment firms that report for their establishments. The main purpose is to maintain the Census Bureau's Business Register.
> *When released*: For use within the Census Bureau.
> *Key variables*: Details about firm ownership, whether firm leases 50% or more of its workforce from a professional employer organization, lists of establishments with establishment-level data on payroll, number of employees by pay period, activity code that "best describes" the activity, and principal products or services. The data are used to maintain the Business Register and provide key source data for County Business Patterns reports and other statistical series.

differences across groups of workers defined by difference in educational attainment, age, and gender. However, the retail transformation is bringing substantial changes to the workforce, with large increases in workers with high-end programming and data analysis skills that support e-commerce. New research in labor economics is investigating ways to measure the skill shifts related to such changes by looking at changes in the tasks involved rather than the educational attainment, age, and gender of the workforce.

ADDITIONAL DATA SOURCES

In addition to the primary data sources described previously, federal data sources also include secondary data products: estimates prepared by federal agencies to illuminate economic concepts such as productivity and the national accounts. Two of these, the BEA Industry Accounts and the BLS BEA Integrated Industry-Level Production Account, are summarized in the first two sections below. The third section describes private and other non-federal data sources, including commercially produced data for purchase, data derived from web-scraping, and credit card data.

BEA Industry Accounts

BEA's industry economic accounts, which are presented both in an input-output framework and as annual output by industry, provide a detailed view of the interrelationships between U.S. producers and users and the contribution made to production across industries.[36] Data products include

- *GDP by industry*, which measures industries' performance and their contributions to GDP;
- *gross output by industry*, principally a measure of sales or revenue from production for most industries, although it is measured as sales or revenue less cost of goods sold for margin industries like wholesale and retail;
- *input-output accounts*, a data set showing how industries interact with each other and with the rest of the economy; and
- *employment by industry*, which measures the nation's number of full- and part-time workers as well as the self-employed.

BEA provides further detail about its input-output accounts:[37] *Supply tables* show the total value of goods and services available in the domestic economy, including those produced by foreign as well as domestic industries. *Use tables* show how the supply of goods and services is used, including domestic purchases by industries, individuals, and government and exports to foreign purchasers. *Requirements tables* summarize the full supply chain by showing how production relies on both direct and indirect inputs. For example, flour is a direct input for a baker, while wheat (used in the production of flour) is an indirect input for the same baker. The requirements tables can be used to analyze the economic repercussions of a natural disaster or other event that changes spending patterns.

Of special interest to this study are the input-output tables, released in November of each year. The input-output accounts are represented in detailed tables showing how industries interact with each other and the rest of the economy. The input-output data, which provide information on 71 industry categories (including 4 in retail, 1 in wholesale, 7 in transportation, and 1 in warehousing), are updated each year. Detailed benchmark input-output statistics, which are further subdivided into 405 industries, are produced roughly every 5 years.

BLS-BEA Integrated Industry-Level Production Account (KLEMS)

During the panel's workshop, Jon Samuels (BEA) told the panel that the new BLS-BEA Integrated Industry-Level Production Accounts (ILPAs)[38]

---

[36] See https://www.bea.gov/data/economic-accounts/industry.

[37] See https://www.bea.gov/resources/learning-center/what-to-know-industries.

[38] A reference for the official BEA-BLS ILPA work is here: https://www.nber.org/papers/w22453.pdf. BEA-BLS have done research work to extend the account back to 1947. See https://www.sciencedirect.com/science/article/pii/B9780128175965000111.

were designed with the intention of capturing innovation and the importance of the trade sectors in aggregate productivity growth (Eldridge et al., 2020; Jorgenson, Ho, and Samuels, 2016). These productivity measures use as the numerator the BEA output measures (gross output and value added), which are consistent with GDP. They make use of the KLEMS approach to compute the input measures. Samuels cited work by Jorgenson, Ho, and Samuels (2016) as describing the approach that has been incorporated into the new BLS-BEA account, but noted that the paper only covers 1987 forward. At a minimum, these accounts may provide information useful to this project, with any proposed satellite account building on this prior joint work, rather than duplicating it.

As described by BEA,[39]

> the ILPA is an ongoing collaboration between BEA and BLS to measure disaggregated prices and quantities of industry outputs and inputs consistent with accounts that measure GDP by industry. The ILPA account includes information on 63 industries that span the total economy. One of its main advantages is that on the input side it is based on disaggregated measures, including about 170 different types of workers by industry (to account for skill mix across industries) and about 100 types of capital assets, including inventories and land (to account for differences in marginal productivities of capital assets). It also uses all the detail on intermediate inputs that underlies BEA annual GDP by industry accounts. This input detail allows for more accurate measures of multifactor productivity growth by industry.[40]

Growth accounting (Jorgenson and Griliches, 1967) provides a method for using the estimates in the integrated industry-level production account to estimate how factors of production contribute to aggregate economic growth. Gollop, Fraumeni, and Jorgenson (1987) showed how to do this at the industry level, and this account uses that basic approach.

The integrated industry-level production account decomposes growth in industry gross output into contributions from growth in intermediate inputs, capital, labor, and multifactor productivity. Similarly, the account decomposes growth in aggregate economy value added into the separate contributions from industries' growth in capital, labor, and multifactor productivity. Data on gross output and intermediate inputs by industry are drawn from BEA statistics on GDP by industry, while data on capital and labor inputs come primarily from the BLS productivity program. Total capital and labor compensation by industry are controlled to match estimates of value added by industry from BEA. Labor, capital, and intermediate inputs

---

[39] See https://www.bea.gov/resources/learning-center/what-to-know-industries.
[40] See https://apps.bea.gov/scb/2020/04-april/0420-integrated-industry-level-production.htm.

are adjusted to account for changes in composition over time. Growth in multifactor productivity is defined residually as the difference between industry output growth and the sum of the share-weighted growth in industry inputs of intermediates, capital, and labor.

Data are provided under the following headings: sector (21 NAICS codes), summary (71 codes), underlying summary (138 groups), and detailed (405 groups, but only available every 5 years). For retail, summary includes three 3-digit codes plus one aggregate for retail and six 3-digit codes for transportation. The underlying summary tables include 11 additional codes for wholesale, 6 additional 3-digit codes for retail, and 2 additional 3-digit codes for transportation. The most recent data release occurred on March 2, 2020.

During the workshop, Samuels noted that under the current NAICS classifications, retail and services are comingled; for example, 30 percent of Motor Vehicle Retailing is under services, as is 12 percent of Restaurant Food and Beverages. He noted that the total factor productivity accounts can be used to analyze these things, and can also be used to split the output of industries by commodity when there is joint production.

Private-Sector and Nonfederal Data

The Census Bureau's Economic Surveys and Economic Census and BLS's statistical collections, some of which were described earlier in this chapter, form the building blocks of the federal economic statistics program. Because of their limitations, however, particularly concerning timeliness and granularity, these surveys and collections are being augmented with private-sector and alternative data sources. Some of the most promising of these alternative sources are scanner data (available for purchase from the private sector), credit card transactions or bank data, and web scraping, each discussed below.

Private retailers and manufacturers have a long history of collecting consumer data, often for market research purposes. Proprietary data are collected, owned, and made available by commercial firms. Granularity is among the strengths of scanner data, and some data are available on a weekly basis. At the same time, these data are collected for marketing or other purposes, are not nationally representative, and are not well documented, and store coverage is not equal across all geographic areas.

Data originating from commercial and alternative sources provide information assets not available elsewhere. Attributes may include timeliness, granularity, geographic distribution, longitudinal information, and cross-time measures. At the same time, hurdles to the use of commercial and alternative data sources include access issues; bias in coverage and representation; perpetually dynamic algorithms; lack of documentation and transparency; fake data and bots; limited scope of organic data sources; and privacy concerns. One of the challenges with the use of any outside data source is determining its quality and coverage, which are key to understanding how the data can best be used. (See NASEM [2020], pp. 76-79, for more detail on challenges.)

Scanner Data

Horrigan (2013) reported that BLS has explored the use of scanner data for many years. The most extensive use he reported was undertaken as comparative research between the CPI and the scanner and associated household panel data from Nielsen. There are two types of scanner data available: data that originate from retail establishments (retail scanner data, such as InfoScan, IRI Worldwide) and data that originate from consumers (household panel and scanner data, such as IRI Worldwide's Consumer Network and Nielsen's Homescan).

The following discussion of scanner data draws heavily on NASEM (2020, pp. 68-70). Retail "scanner data capture transactions for purchased products with a Universal Product Code (UPC) on their labels, as well as random-weight products such as fruits and vegetables" (NASEM, 2020, p. 68). The retail data include store information, including store name and corporate parent, address, and retail outlet type. "Granularity is among the strengths of scanner data" (NASEM, 2020, p. 69), some of which are available on a weekly basis. For each consumer store purchase, "scanner devices can detect and record exactly which products are purchased, the number of items, total dollars spent after discounts (if any), and total gross amount (before discount)" (NASEM, 2020, p. 68). With this information, "researchers can infer the average price paid as the ratio between dollars spent and units purchased, since many retailers do not share individual-level purchase prices with the data aggregators (Nielsen and IRI) but prefer to share average prices within a store or across geographic areas. This means the price data are not individual prices but are averages" (NASEM, 2020, p. 68).

"From the perspective of the firms IRI and Nielsen, store data are seen as a census. Whether or not this is accurate, their methods do not treat these sales data as a sample, and data available for purchase may include only those stores that have agreed to share their data. *Infoscan*, for example, does not include all large retailers (e.g., Costco is not included)" (NASEM, 2020, p. 68, footnote 32).

"The National Consumer Panel, a joint venture by Nielsen and IRI, is used by both these firms in their household panel data products. It comprises more than 120,000 households, which provide information on their demographic characteristics in addition to purchase information (NASEM, 2020, p. 70). "Unlike the retail scanner data collected at check-out, household scanner data are collected using hand-held scanning devices provided to participating households or using a mobile cellphone app. In this way, purchases can be captured for the panel of households. Again, this source includes products with barcodes" (NASEM, 2020, p. 70).

The Economic Research Service (ERS) uses the Nielsen and IRI data (both retail scanner data and household consumption and scanner data) in addition to other purchased data as an integral part of its Consumer Food Data Program (NASEM, 2020). Brent Nieman and Joseph Vavra (2019) use Nielsen Homescan data to investigate changes in consumer shopping over the last 15 years. Scanner data and credit card transactions data have the potential to improve price indices by adjusting for the long lags between incorporation of the Economic Census data into the Census Bureau's data program. Scanner data, in particular, are especially rich and available for the retail trade sector.

Credit Card Transactions, Bank Data, and Payroll Processor Microdata

One of the more exciting new applications of credit card data to improve the timeliness of estimates is BEA's advance estimates of GDP for 2020, undertaken to try to capture the impact of COVID-19 on the economy. As noted in news releases, advance estimates are based on source data that are subject to updates. Much of the data used in these advance estimates is from the monthly and quarterly surveys that are part of the Census Bureau's Economic Surveys. However, BEA also reported that its "assumptions were based on a variety of sources, most notably: private high-frequency credit card transactions data to better capture shifts in consumer spending, news reports on reopenings, and industry and trade association reports, that include volume data, such as health care patient visits and traveler throughput. More information on the source data and BEA assumptions that underlie the second-quarter estimate is shown in the 'Key Source Data and Assumptions' table on the BEA Website."[41]

Cajner and colleagues (2018) show that high-frequency private payroll microdata can help forecast labor market conditions, noting that payroll employment is the most reliable real-time indicator of the business cycle. In their example, they demonstrate that using payroll microdata substantially improved forecast accuracy for current month employment and revisions to the BLS Current Employment Statistics.

Using anonymized transactions data from a large electronic payments technology company, Aladangady and colleagues (2019) created daily estimates of retail spending at detailed geographies. When aggregated to the national level, they found that these estimates had a pattern of monthly

---

[41] From https://www.bea.gov/sites/default/files/2020-07/tech2q20_adv.pdf.

growth rates similar to that found in the official Census statistics. The daily estimates were available a few days after the transactions, and the authors provided historical estimates from 2010. They suggested that such daily estimates might be particularly useful during times of stress, such as hurricanes. Other examples include Mian, Rao, and Sufi (2013) using credit card company data, and Farrell and Greig (2015) using accounts from a large bank.

In most of these studies, the source data were purchased or use of the data was granted through agreements. Collaborations between the government and the larger Internet-related companies in private industry, many of which have assembled massive data sets, might fruitfully expand the data available for the study of the retail trade transformation.

Web Scraping

Web scraping is the practice of extracting data from websites, typically through the use of a software program that simulates human exploration. One of the best-known examples of web scraping is the Billion Prices Project at MIT,[42] which constructed daily price indexes for several countries using web scraping techniques to convert posted Internet prices of products to create a new daily version of a consumer price index for 22 countries (Cavallo and Rigobon, 2016).

The Bureau of Justice Statistics conducted a pilot project using web-scraped data from online articles to try to improve estimates for arrest-related deaths, finding that the "open-source methodology alone identifies the majority of law enforcement homicides, but agency surveys aid in identifying deaths by other causes (e.g., accidents, suicides, and natural causes)."[43]

While web-scraping has great potential, it also creates policy challenges for federal statistical agencies. Unresolved questions include whether information on a company's website can be considered publicly available data and how confidentiality protections should be applied. Policy to date has guided statistical agencies to secure permission from companies before web-scraping data from their websites.

Other Sources

Other alternative data sources include information from trade associations and commercial data on establishments. The National Establishment Time Series (NETS) is extracted from Dun and Bradstreet and available

---

[42] See http://bpp.mit.edu.
[43] See https://www.bjs.gov/index.cfm?ty=pbdetail&iid=6626.

from Wold Associates.[44] The NPD Group provides retail tracking data including firm and store/product-level sales data.[45]

> CONCLUSION 3-11: Private-sector data, such as scanner data, might support capturing both quantities and prices of purchases to estimate the price effect of consumers moving between retail outlets.
>
> CONCLUSION 3-12: Private-sector, credit card, and payroll processing data have been used to provide more timely information about economic output, prices, and input that could potentially be used to provide more timely estimates for labor productivity in the retail-related sector, though issues about the representativeness of those data will need to be addressed.
>
> CONCLUSION 3-13: A collaboration between the government and larger Internet-related private companies has the potential to vastly expand the types of data available to study the transformation in retail trade and may support detailed analysis by population subgroup.

---

[44] See http://maryannfeldman.web.unc.edu/data-sources/longitudinal-databases/national-establishment-time-series-nets.

[45] See https://www.npd.com/wps/portal/npd/us/solutions/tracking-services/retail-tracking.

4

Toward a Retail Satellite Account

This chapter starts with a summary of what satellite accounts are and then describes optional approaches that might be considered for a satellite account to describe the broader retail sector. It goes on to describe existing satellite accounts and how some of their features might illuminate the development of a retail-related satellite account.

Information concerning satellite accounts was derived from the relevant literature and, most importantly, from the workshop organized by the panel to gather information. This included a background paper on satellite accounts in Canada produced by Philip Smith, *Satellite Accounting in Canada* (Smith, 2020). The fourth workshop session, titled, "Toward a BLS Satellite Account for Retail,"[1] was of key importance to this discussion. Other sessions relevant to the discussion were the third session, "Data: Availability, Needs, Discrepancies and Gaps,"[2] and the fifth session, "Uses of Bottom-up in Measuring Employment and Productivity."[3] The latter two sessions were also discussed in Chapter 3.

---

[1] Discussants included Brian Chansky, BLS; Tina Highfill, BEA; Philip Smith, Statistics Canada (retired); and Marshall Reinsdorf, International Monetary Fund; as well as panel members Leonard Nakamura and Carol Corrado.

[2] Discussants included Ken Robertson, BLS; Jon D. Samuels, BEA; Matthew Russell, BEA; Ian Thomas, Census Bureau; and Edward Watkins, Census Bureau. The moderator was panel member Wesley Yung, Statistics Canada.

[3] Presentation by panel members Teresa Fort, Dartmouth College; and John Haltiwanger, University of Maryland.

WHAT ARE SATELLITE ACCOUNTS AND HOW ARE THEY USED?

Satellite accounts are described by Eurostat as accounts that provide "a framework for exploring some aspect of the economy that is linked to the System of National Accounts (SNA), allowing attention to be focused on a certain field or aspect of economic and social life in the context of national accounts."[4] Eurostat cites as common examples satellite accounts that focus on the environment, tourism, or unpaid household work. As Philip Smith details in his background paper, over the last three decades this method of accounting has gradually become popular around the globe. It first emerged in the 1980s as an idea, was set out formally in 1993, and was fully established in 2008 (Smith, 2020, p. 1). It is described more fully in Box 4-1.

Smith regards the SNA as "an enormously successful framework for describing the world economy and the national and sub-national economies," while noting that "no system can be all things to all people and the SNA certainly has its limitations" (Smith, 2020, p. 1). Its central concept, gross domestic product (GDP), is perhaps the best known and most widely used economic statistic available. Smith goes on to say:

> Satellite accounts offer a means of borrowing some of the best features of the international SNA while giving freedom to depart from some of its restrictions. Often people want to know the size of a particular activity, such as tourism or the digital economy, in relation to the total market economy. Satellite accounts provide a way of determining this. Alternative valuations can be adopted and the production boundary can be redefined. Product and industry classes can be recombined in other ways that may be more convenient for some purposes. Alternative (more familiar) vocabulary can be adopted. And all of this can be done while linking directly into the large, internally consistent and carefully curated databases offered by the SNA. (Smith, 2020, p. 2)

Smith also cautions that "there are costs as well as benefits from moving away from the international standard SNA into satellite accounts. One country's satellite account may not be easily comparable to another's, and it may not be possible to aggregate satellite accounts from different countries. The Organisation for Economic Co-operation and Development (OECD) and the United Nations are working to encourage some standardization, but standardization takes time and also conflicts with one of the major benefits of satellite accounting: its flexibility. In addition, satellite accounts are

---

[4] See https://ec.europa.eu/eurostat/statistics-explained/index.php/Glossary:Satellite_account#:~:text=Satellite%20accounts%20provide%20a%20framework,tourism%2C%20or%20unpaid%20household%20work, page 1. This link is to introductory lecture notes on satellite accounts by Eurostat.

> **BOX 4-1**
> **System of National Accounts**
>
> The System of National Accounts (SNA) is the internationally agreed standard set of recommendations on how to compile measures of economic activity. The SNA describes a coherent, consistent, and integrated set of macroeconomic accounts in the context of a set of internationally agreed concepts, definitions classifications, and accounting rules. In addition, the SNA provides an overview of economic processes, recording how production is distributed among consumers, businesses, government, and foreign nations.
>
> Consequently, the national accounts are one of the building blocks of macroeconomic statistics, forming a basis for economic analysis and policy formulation. The SNA is intended for use by all countries.
>
> SOURCE: See https://unstats.un.org/unsd/nationalaccount/sna.asp#:~:text=.

more vulnerable to political influence, since they often depend on outside financial and other support from their main clients" (Smith, 2020, p. 21).

A recent survey administered by Statistics Canada for the United Nations Economic Commission for Europe (UNECE) covered more than 80 countries and identified 241 satellite accounts. It was part of the work program of the Conference of European Statisticians, and its main objectives were to determine the extent of satellite accounting around the world and explore why and in what directions satellite accounting studies are increasing. According to Smith,

> The UNECE survey found that the most common topics addressed were tourism, environment and health. Primary reasons mentioned for developing these accounts were (1) giving greater prominence to a particular activity, (2) bringing more detailed statistics to an activity than are directly available in the core national accounts, and (3) extending the conceptual boundaries in the core national accounts for production, consumption and/or assets. (Smith, 2020, p. 2)

It may also be useful to consider how Eurostat, the statistical agency of the European Union, defines satellite accounts in its online glossary:

> Satellite accounts are one way in which the SNA may be adapted to meet differing circumstances and needs. They are closely linked to the main system but are not bound to employ exactly the same concepts or restrict themselves to data expressed in monetary terms. Satellite accounts are intended for special purposes such as monitoring the community's health

or the state of the environment. They may also be used to explore new methodologies and to work out new accounting procedures that, when fully developed and accepted, might become absorbed into the main system over time. Satellite accounts can meet specific data needs by providing more detail, by rearranging concepts from the central framework or by providing supplementary information. They can range from simple tables to an extended set of accounts in special areas like [for example,] environment or education."[5]

An important question in setting up such an account is how to ensure that it is a place to experiment with new data and methodology while maintaining acceptable levels of error from a data user's perspective. It is, by definition, a derived data product measuring selected economic concepts. The proposed development of a retail-related satellite account has a data quality objective: to improve the relevance of employment and productivity measures for retail.

Another critical aspect of data quality is transparency. This argues for keeping users of the satellite account engaged and informed, and for providing them with information so that they can determine whether the data are fit for their use and provide feedback to further the development of the account.

At the workshop, Steve Landefeld, former director of BEA, which has a long history of developing satellite accounts, noted that it is most important to address the underlying data from a statistical viewpoint, such as standard errors and replicability, as part of preparing such an account for production. In BEA's experience, useful questions to ask in addressing this include the following: Can this be done in the new account with the same data quality as the current employment, productivity, or GDP? Does the new account get the trend right? If yes, does it get whether growth is high or low right?

In its own development of satellite accounts, BEA employs the following criteria to assess data quality (see Box 4-2).

AUDIENCES FOR A RETAIL RELATED SATELLITE ACCOUNT AND MEASURES OF EMPLOYMENT AND PRODUCTIVITY

A primary concern among potential users of employment and productivity data is to be able to capture the transformational shifts in the sector, which is the same concern that has motivated BLS to consider a satellite account. Primary users of current statistics on the retail sector want to understand how retail productivity is changing and how it contributes

---

[5]See https://ec.europa.eu/eurostat/statistics-explained/index.php/Glossary:Satellite_account#:~:text=Satellite%20accounts%20provide%20a%20framework,tourism%2C%20or%20unpaid%20household%20work, p. 1.

> **BOX 4-2**
> **Evaluation Criteria**
>
> - How close are they to BEA's mission and expertise?
> - How relevant and useful are they to customers, experts, policy makers, business users, investors, Congress, and the Administration?
> - How often do they need to be produced?
> - What are the resource costs to begin regular production? (And benefits relative to core research)
> - What is the methodology and what is the availability of source data?
>   —Accuracy, timeliness, relevance, objectivity, and use of economic theory and methods
> - Why should BEA rather than others produce these accounts?
> - How successfully can BEA vet and roll out the alternative accounts?

to overall productivity; a retail-related satellite account could provide a perspective on these questions that better reflects the transformational shifts in the sector.

These primary potential users of newly formulated estimates for employment and productivity include the following:

- *Monetary, administration, and congressional authorities,* who rely on data tracking changes in retail trade productivity. Monetary authorities use them in making projections of sustainable growth when formulating monetary policy. Administration and congressional authorities use them to assess sources of growth in the economy for making budget projections. For example, Triplett and Bosworth (2004, abstract) analyzed services sector productivity, including communications, transportation, and the wholesale and retail trade, demonstrating the role of information technology in accelerating services sector productivity. The authors also highlighted the importance of making improvements within the U.S. statistical system to provide the more accurate and relevant measures essential for analyzing productivity and economic growth.
- *Federal, state, and local government officials,* who use federal data to assess issues related to tax policies and government regulations. For example, retail trade data are key to understanding the impact of COVID-19 and policies to assist afflicted workers.
- *Professional and trade associations,* which use federal data to represent the retail industry in discussions about such areas as taxation and regulation.

- *Institutional investors*, which use federal data to provide a reality check on the short- and long-term prospects for an industry.
- *Individual companies*, which use federal data on retail trade to provide information on industry trends as a reality check for expansions, mergers and acquisitions, and other long-term investments.

In addition to these primary uses of the newly formulated employment and productivity measures, a satellite account could support more detailed analyses that would benefit particular users and potentially lead to long-term improvements in the relevant employment and productivity statistics.

- Researchers use federal data to identify economic relationships that are not directly reflected in the reported statistics, such as contrasts related to firm size or between domestic and foreign-owned establishments.
- Macroeconomists are interested in measures that capture the dynamics of broad sectors of the economy.
- Individual retail companies may be interested in using the newly formulated measures in benchmarking themselves against the industry.

In summary, a satellite account provides a useful and flexible mechanism for studying the expanded retail-related sector.

CONCLUSION 4-1: A satellite account provides a framework to explore a specific aspect of the economy that is linked to the System of National Accounts while deviating in ways that help address important questions about that aspect of the economy. These deviations may involve grouping or valuing economic activities in different ways than the national accounts or providing more detailed statistics than are provided in the national accounts.

DEFINING A RETAIL-SUPPORTING SECTOR

Box 4-3 summarizes the options that were provided in advance of the workshop to participants in the session titled, "Toward a BLS Satellite Account for Retail." These options were initially presented in BLS (2020) to stimulate thought about how a satellite account might be structured. BLS observed that other options should also be considered.

Figure 4-1a is a diagram with a comparison of the *distributional* and *retail-related* sectors. It illustrates that these two options are related only to those NAICS codes that best describe the establishments within each option, not to the classification of their enterprises. *Distributional* is the simpler concept since it includes only major-sector NAICS designations.

> **BOX-4-3**
> **Four Alternative Definitions of a Retail-Related Sector**
>
> The fundamental issue raised by the transformations in retail and the BLS charge to the panel involves the increasing integration of a range of wholesale, warehouse, and delivery functions into the services provided by retailers: here are four options for defining a retail-related satellite account.
>
> 1. *Distributional retail* would include much or all of wholesale, retail, warehousing, and freight transportation. It might be defined as follows: All establishments engaged in the business of distributing goods from manufacturers, agriculture, resource extraction, and importers to users (including both firms and final consumers). It might include the following NAICS sectors: retail (44-45), wholesale (42), and transportation and warehousing (48-49).
> 2. A *retail-supporting* sector would include retail trade plus some elements of transportation, warehousing, wholesale trade, and business services that serve retail trade firms. It could be defined as all establishments in retail trade and establishments in specific NAICS codes in other sectors that primarily serve retail activities or customers. It might include retail (44, 45) plus the more detailed NAICS codes from 42, 48, 49, and 56 that are specifically related to retail. It would likely require splitting some NAICS codes into retail-trade supporting and other.
> 3. A *retail-controlled* sector would include retail trade establishments and other establishments, regardless of how classified, in enterprises primarily engaged in retail trade. Includes retail trade establishments (NAICS 42) as well as other establishments in enterprises classified into retail trade.
> 4. Finally, an *enterprise-based retail trade* sector would include all establishments that are part of enterprises or firms primarily engaged in retail trade. Includes all enterprises classified in retail trade and their establishments, regardless of how classified.
>
> SOURCE: Bureau of Labor Statistics (2020).

Figure 4-1b compares the *retail-controlled* and *enterprise-based* sectors. Both of these options make use of the classification of an enterprise as part of the definition. Here *enterprise-based* is the simpler concept, since it includes only those establishments located within a retail enterprise.

Discussants observed that a *distributional retail* definition may be overly broad even though it would be the most straightforward to implement from a data point of view. However, starting with a distributional account and moving toward a version of *retail-supporting* may be a good strategy, because starting with the simplest option helps to inform next steps and develop expertise. It could be called a case study to get initial

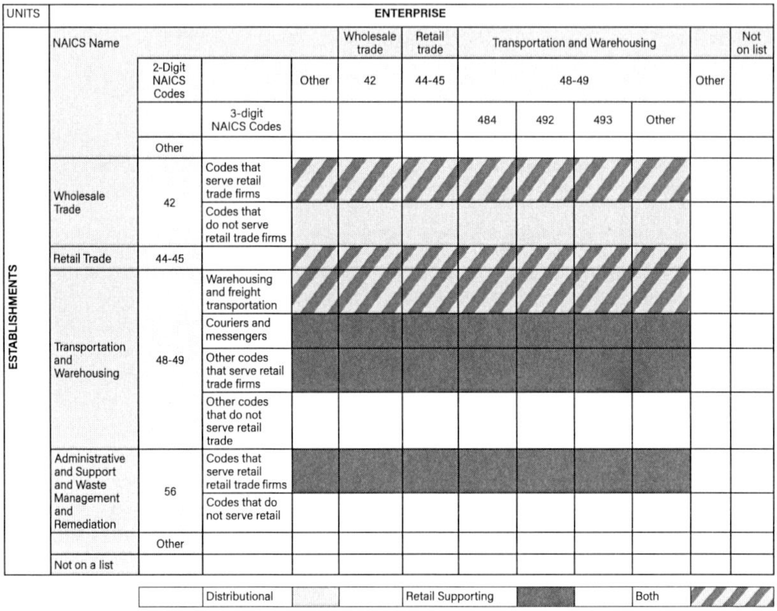

80 A SATELLITE ACCOUNT TO MEASURE THE RETAIL TRANSFORMATION

FIGURE 4-1a Comparison of distributional and retail-supporting industry codes.

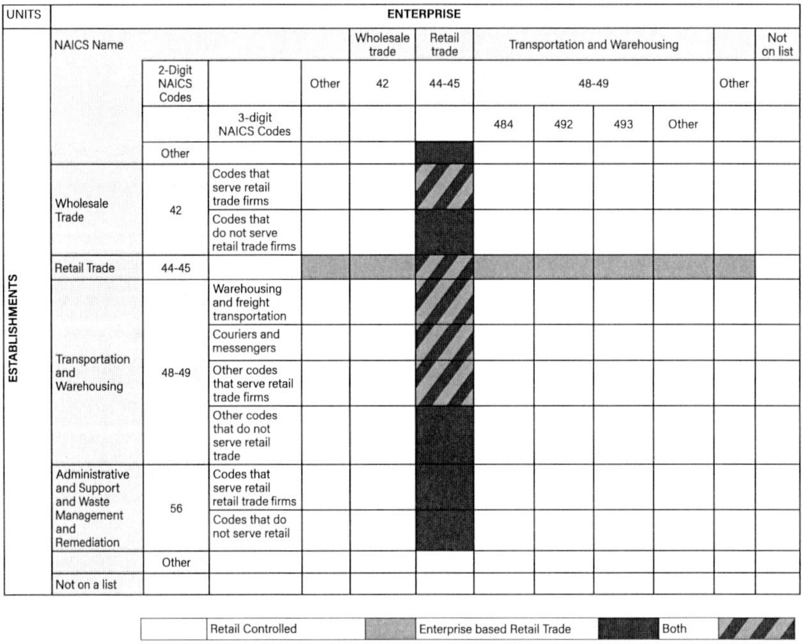

FIGURE 4-1b Comparison of retail-controlled and enterprise-based industry codes.

results out so that users could provide input. One difficulty of this may be separating passenger transportation services from goods transportation, particularly for air travel.

There are three major disadvantages of *retail-controlled* and *retail-enterprise-based* options. First, BLS does not have the information to develop enterprise-based statistics comparable to those produced by the Census Bureau. Second, an enterprise-based retail trade account would be outside the NAICS framework. Third, the sector definition would depend on vertical integration. Enterprise classifications, especially among complex firms, can change from year to year. This alone would make defining accounts based on enterprise classification undesirable for tracking trends. Additionally, discussants observed that the retail-controlled definition seemed too narrow, even though an enterprise-based definition might be of interest to data users.

Data issues with these two options are due to the fact that the data on enterprise classifications and links to their establishments are available only for approved projects through the Census Bureau at Federal Statistical Research Data Centers (FSRDCs). While data are available to approved outside researchers, obtaining a new data product for use in a satellite account would require collaboration, interagency agreements, and time.

> CONCLUSION 4-2: None of the four options on which to base a satellite account is perfect as it stands; however, a definition based on *retail supporting* is closest to what is needed according to the statement of work and most practical. Elements of the broader option, *distributional*, will also need to be incorporated into the newly defined *retail-supporting* sector, such as auxiliary establishments and parts of other industries, such as computing, intangibles, leasing, and importing. Identifying the precise definition(s) to be used for the *retail-supporting* sector will require exploration and experimentation.

> CONCLUSION 4-3: To better understand the changes in retail-trade-related industries, a collaborative effort between the Bureau of Labor Statistics, Bureau of Economic Analysis, and Census Bureau staff could make use of microdata as a laboratory to better understand many of the complicated aspects of developing a retail-related satellite account. The purpose would be to use the concepts and data to gain a better understanding of key issues, such as assessing the structural changes associated with the retail trade transformation by size of enterprise; understanding the role of auxiliaries and other nonretail establishments within retail trade enterprises; and assessing data gaps and approaches to solving them.

Splitting NAICS Codes into Retail- and Nonretail-Supporting

As described under "retail-supporting" in Box 4-3, implementing a satellite account will likely require estimating the portion of the output and the portion of the input under some detailed NAICS codes in wholesale, transportation, warehousing, and others that are retail-related versus nonretail-related.

In some cases, the contrasts between detailed NAICS codes can provide an indication of whether an industry is likely to support the retail sector. For industries that support several sectors, such as wholesale trade and transportation, there is some information available about the portion of output directed to retail in the NAICS classification system. Four-digit NAICS codes for wholesale trade often differentiate between consumer products (e.g., groceries, furniture and home furnishing, motor vehicles, apparel, beer, and wine) and producer products (e.g., chemicals, farm raw materials, and raw metals and materials).

A NAICS designation alone is not always sufficient to identify the contribution of retail-related establishments that partly support retail and partly support something else. For example, NAICS 481112 comprises establishments primarily engaged in providing air transportation of cargo (not passengers) over regular routes and on regular schedules. However, this cargo transportation may also support retail, wholesale, mail delivery, or something else.

Beyond the NAICS codes of the establishments themselves, data from the Census Bureau's Economic Surveys provide some information about the commodities an establishment deals in as part of its sources of revenue.

Canada's satellite accounts usually rely on Statistics Canada's input-output tables. These satellite accounts typically rearrange information from those tables and add in additional detail from other sources. Statistical products based on input-output tables may have substantial delays in publication, so satellite accounts also need to be supplemented with more current indicators and projections.

Bureau of Economic Analysis (BEA) satellite accounts are also typically developed from BEA input-output tables.[6] These accounts are developed by first looking through the list of 5,000 goods and services to determine which are in-scope for the new project. Then BEA seeks to determine whether the whole commodity is within scope or only part of the commodity is. As

---

[6] See https://www.bea.gov/resources/learning-center/what-to-know-industries. Input-output data are updated each year and provide information on 71 industry categories. Detailed benchmark input-output statistics, produced roughly every 5 years, are further subdivided into 405 industries. Data sources include the Economic Census, including a special tabulation on auxiliaries, the Annual Retail Trade Survey, and other sources. The manual for input-output accounts is found here: https://apps.bea.gov/papers/pdf/IOmanual_092906.pdf.

described in the next section ("Existing Satellite Accounts"), one example is bicycles for the outdoor recreation account. As determined from an outside source survey, 93 percent of people who buy bicycles purchase them for outdoor recreation, the others may be purchasing them for business use, such as courier work.

Input-output tables (in particular, the use tables) provide estimates of the proportion of output in services such as wholesale and trucking that are attributable to retail and the shares of intermediate inputs of goods and services purchased by the retail trade. They also provide estimates for changes in these proportions over time. The BEA input-output table starts with a gross output measure (gross margins for trade industries and gross sales for other industries) and uses the relationships found in the input-output table to determine a value-added number and then an employment number. This distribution of intermediate goods and services purchased by the retail trade could be used to develop a definition of retail-supporting industries, though it might not have the full NAICS code detail needed.

While this provides one way to identify the split between retail and nonretail output, the proportions are unlikely to be the same for the labor that goes into those categories. It was observed that questions have been raised about the net impact of e-commerce on jobs and employment. Estimating how many people are working in retail and retail-supporting sectors, as well as estimating the net change in jobs and pay, would be very helpful by itself and useful for measuring productivity.

Estimation of the split between retail-related and nonretail-related inputs will likely require some creative use of alternative data sources. Some companies[7] may have internal worker-level data about what workers were doing—such as handling aircraft engines versus clothing. There may also be trade associations of delivery firms that collect this type of information.

> CONCLUSION 4-4: The retail-supporting sector definition will likely require splitting the currently measured input and output for some North American Industry Classification System codes into retail-related and "other." Options are available for splitting retail-related outputs. Using existing Bureau of Economic Analysis' input-output tables as well as those available in the Bureau of Labor Statistics/BEA Integrated Labor Productivity Account may provide a start, and approaches that use existing data on commodities transported from the Commodities Flow Survey are also likely to be useful. However, this account will also need to develop new methods and data to estimate the split in input between retail-related and other, which will likely require experimentation and the development of new data sources.

---

[7]Reported by Richard Phillips at the workshop.

CONCLUSION 4-5: It is important to start with a relatively simple sector definition to develop expertise and communicate with users. The distributional option was mentioned as a possible starting point, but it was viewed as overly broad. Another useful starting point might be to start from the list of North American Industry Classification System codes to be included in the expanded retail-supporting option, identifying those that are entirely retail-supporting or partly retail-supporting. An account that includes only those codes that are entirely retail-supporting and an account that includes all codes with some retail-supporting activity provide upper and lower bounds for what might be gained by a careful development of estimates for splitting the input and output of industries that are partly retail-supporting. The distribution of intermediate goods and services purchased by retail trade as measured in the Bureau of Economic Analysis input-output tables could also be used to start the development of a definition of retail-supporting industries.

The discussion of satellite accounts reinforced the importance of filling the data gaps identified in Chapter 3. The major new data gap identified during the discussion in Chapter 4 is the need to identify the proportion of input and output in selected NAICS codes that is retail-related, along with the key observation that the proportion is likely not the same for input and output. Developing the split for input will likely require new data sources and approaches.

It is possible to start the project using the simple assumption that the input and output can be split using the same proportion, but it will be important to develop data to either confirm that assumption or to replace it with better estimates.

EXISTING SATELLITE ACCOUNTS WITH POTENTIALLY USEFUL FEATURES

BEA has prepared many of the satellite accounts in the United States.[8] Similarly, Statistics Canada has prepared most of the satellite accounts in Canada (which are summarized in Smith, 2020). The workshop discussion identified the BEA satellite accounts discussed next as having features that may prove valuable in the design and implementation of a retail-related satellite e-account.

---

[8] See https://www.bea.gov/data/special-topics for links to the BEA satellite accounts.

BEA states[9] that it

> ... developed the *digital economy satellite account* to better capture the effects of fast-changing technologies on the U.S. economy and on global supply chains. The project calculates the digital economy's contribution to U.S. GDP and improved measures of high-tech goods and services, and it offers a more complete picture of international trade. Other goals are to advance research for digital goods and services, the sharing economy, and free digital content, and to explore economic measures beyond GDP to better understand Americans' well-being. BEA includes in its definition of the digital economy three major types of goods and services:
>
> 1. *infrastructure*, or the basic physical materials and organizational arrangements that support the existence and use of computer networks and the digital economy; primarily information and communications technology (ICT) goods and services;
> 2. *e-commerce*, or the remote sale of goods and services over computer networks; and
> 3. *priced digital services*, or those services related to computing and communication and that are performed for a fee charged to the consumer.

The BEA digital economy satellite account already addresses some retail areas and illustrates a flexible use of sources to allocate different industries into digital and nondigital pieces. This account required the organization of a new sector from the ground up. The OECD has guidance for developing a digital economy satellite account that may be worth reviewing in developing a satellite account for retail trade.[10]

As summarized by BEA,[11]

> BEA developed a set of supplemental statistics called the *health care satellite account* to better measure spending trends and treatment prices. This satellite account measures U.S. health care spending by the diseases being treated (for example, cancer or diabetes) instead of by the types of goods and services purchased (such as doctor's office visits or drugs). At the same time, BEA continues to produce the traditional goods-and-services health care estimates that are part of its core statistics, such as GDP. Within this satellite account, there are two different sets of disease-based statistics. One version uses data from the Medical Expenditure Panel Survey, the only nationally representative survey that contains detailed expenditure information by disease. BEA calls this the MEPS Account. Because of its relatively small sample size, the MEPS Account produces more volatile estimates across years. To address this issue, BEA also produces a 'Blended

---

[9] See https://www.bea.gov/data/special-topics/digital-economy.
[10] See https://www.oecd.org/sdd/its/Handbook-on-Measuring-Digital-Trade-Version-1.pdf.
[11] See https://www.bea.gov/data/special-topics/health-care.

Account,' which blends together data from multiple sources, including large claims databases that cover millions of enrollees and billions of claims.

The BEA *outdoor recreation satellite account* "measures the economic activity as well as the sales or receipts generated by outdoor recreational activities, such as fishing and vacation travel by recreational vehicle. These statistics also measure each industry's production of outdoor goods and services and its contribution to U.S. GDP. Industry breakdowns of outdoor employment and compensation are also included."[12]

The BEA outdoor recreation satellite account had to apportion many commodities between "recreation" and "something else," in ways similar to what will be needed in the retail-related satellite account. BEA used about two dozen data sources to do this, including a survey that measured whether purchased bicycles were for recreational or business use. This satellite account may be especially relevant because there was no precedent about how an outdoor recreation sector should be defined, but there were strong views. BEA ended up having two definitions, one narrow and one broad. The outdoor recreation account might be a guide in how to allocate output according to input-output relationships versus outside sources.

Finally, a new satellite account is being developed by BEA, the Small Business Administration, Statistics Canada, and the University of Pennsylvania (Highfill et al., 2020) to better track the *overall growth and relative contributions of small business in the U.S. economy*. A main challenge with this account is identifying the portion of gross output from manufacturing firms attributable to very small businesses. Tina Highfill, of BEA, highlighted this account because some users wanted enterprise-level statistics, which pose data challenges. While some data are available, data on enterprises and their establishments are only available in the Census Bureau's business register, which makes them challenging to access except for approved projects through an FSRDC.

Another set of satellite accounts that may provide guidance on splitting transportation NAICS codes into retail-supporting versus other is the Bureau of Transportation Statistics (BTS) Transportation Satellite Accounts, prepared by BTS in collaboration with BEA.[13]

> **CONCLUSION 4-6:** Several existing Bureau of Economic Analysis satellite accounts may provide useful models for developing a retail satellite account, given the measurement challenges posed by the retail transformation. The digital economy satellite account includes

---

[12] See https://www.bea.gov/data/special-topics/outdoor-recreation.
[13] See https://www.bts.gov/satellite-accounts.

e-commerce and digital services, which are both important aspects of the retail transformation. The health care satellite account involves a reconceptualization of health care spending, which might suggest novel ways to reflect the changing cost structure of retail. The outdoor recreation satellite account addresses the challenge of dividing up statistics from several industries to combine some of them in a new grouping that is useful to the field. The small business satellite account addresses the challenge of identifying establishments of different sizes, which may also be an important way to divide the data for the retail sector.

5

Recommendations for a Retail Satellite Account

In this chapter we review the information provided in the previous chapters and present the panel's recommendations. The statement of task requested the following: a review of the issues related to measuring employment and productivity in retail-related industries, an evaluation of changes in the retail trade landscape and an assessment of how they are impacting measures of employment and productivity, and a review of the existing measures as well as the methodological issues surrounding measurement of these concepts. The panel was asked to determine "if, and how, a satellite account can be designed to capture this retail transformation"; and to comment on (1) the value and specifications for a satellite account for the retail-related sector, (2) ways to identify the proportion of output, employment, and hours outside of retail trade that are directed toward supporting retail trade, and (3) ways to maintain a retail-related satellite account.

The chapter points out how this report addresses the original statement of task by referring back to previous chapters and providing the panel's recommendations.

The overarching recommendation is for the Bureau of Labor Statistics (BLS) to develop a labor productivity satellite account that will enable a fuller understanding and better measurement of the transformation of retail trade. Within this supplementary satellite account, BLS can begin to develop and experiment with new measures, which could feature the following:

- Alternative concepts of output for retail trade, such as gross margins and value-added, that better measure the output and productivity

of retail trade by focusing on the services that retail trade provides rather than on the products they sell;
- Price indexes that better measure changes in the quality of the services retail trade provides rather than the quality of the goods they sell;
- Quality-adjusted measures of labor input, beginning with those already in use in the integrated BLS and Bureau of Economic Analysis (BEA) multifactor productivity estimates;
- Estimates for both the retail sector and the retail-related sector that capture the changing organizational structure of retail trade; and
- Parallel estimates featuring currently used measures based on existing methodologies and source data (gross sales, final goods deflators, and unadjusted labor hours).

The last set of estimates will be key to assessing the new indicators against the existing indicators in their ability to decompose and identify changes in labor productivity due to changes in the organization of retail trade, changes in the services provided by retail trade, changes in the quality of the goods, and changes due to increased labor quality versus labor hours.

MOTIVATION AND OVERARCHING RECOMMENDATIONS

The statement of task asks the panel to evaluate changes in the retail trade landscape, assess how they are impacting measures of employment and productivity in retail-related industries, and determine whether and how a satellite account could be designed to capture this retail transformation. The panel's evaluation of the changes in retail trade industries is presented in Chapter 2, along with a discussion of the measurement challenges this transformation poses (**Conclusions 2-1 and 2-2**). **Conclusion 4-1** summarizes some of the attributes of a satellite account that make it well suited to evaluate the impact of the changes observed in retail trade industries.

One key advantage of a satellite account is its potential to enable experimentation with alternative concepts and more detailed and alternative definitions. In addition to providing a mechanism to study the continuing transformation of retail trade, a satellite account can suggest important additions to data collection and analysis to resolve data gaps. A valuable output of the satellite account might be an updated approach to measuring labor productivity for the main accounts published by BLS, one that could more clearly illustrate the impact of the transformation in retail trade.

CONCLUSION 5-1: A satellite account would be an appropriate and useful vehicle for the Bureau of Labor Statistics to use to study the impact of the transformation in retail trade on employment and

productivity and to develop exploratory measures that describe that transformation.

Development of a retail-related satellite account is best conducted by an interagency team comprising staff from those agencies that have the widest range of expertise and skills needed to address this challenge. As described in Chapter 3, the needed expertise, skills, and data are spread across three separate agencies, including coverage of economic analysis (BEA, BLS, and Census), the development and use of satellite accounts (BEA), and the development and use of data systems and surveys that measure output (those of the Census Bureau) or that measure employment and prices (BLS). The study of the transformation in retail trade is important for a variety of reasons, including the fact that many of the changes in retail trade are also seen in other sectors. It is critically important for the government statistical system to adapt information collection and data systems to measure changing industries.

Models for such a collaborative interagency approach already exist, including the BLS's Collaborative Micro Productivity Project, which developed new data products (Dispersion Statistics on Productivity [DiSP]),[1] and BEA's Integrated BEA GDP-BLS Productivity Account.[2]

RECOMMENDATION 1: The Bureau of Labor Statistics should develop a satellite account for an expanded retail trade sector in collaboration with the Bureau of Economic Analysis and the Census Bureau. Such a team could be formed under the Evidence-Based Policymaking Act to facilitate administrative and collaborative efforts.

Like many ongoing systems, the U.S. Federal Statistical System has not been as nimble in keeping up with industry change as would be desirable. While keeping up with change is never easy, mechanisms are needed to help identify what is important to change and how. As noted in Chapter 2, the retail-related industry is changing fast at the margins, and the near-term future is likely to see substantially new changes beyond those that are currently well-known in the industry.

Due to the COVID-19 pandemic, the diffusion of innovations like e-commerce is accelerating and evolving. Somehow, retail experts from the industry need to be involved to make sure that the measures developed are not just of academic interest but instead are of interest to industry as a whole and are designed to be sensitive to new trends. Industry also has access to new types of data that may provide important new measures

---

[1] See https://www.bls.gov/lpc/productivity-dispersion.htm.
[2] See https://www.bea.gov/data/special-topics/integrated-bea-gdp-bls-productivity-account.

(**Conclusions 3-11, 3-12, and 3-13**). Public-private partnerships or outside technical advisory committees might help decide how some of these measurement challenges can be addressed. One such industry-collaborative project was undertaken under the Federal Economic Statistics Advisory Committee. An older successful example was a collaboration on hedonics for computer products, which was developed with key inputs and analysis from IBM (Cole et al., 1986). The question is how to best involve retail industry experts to help the interagency team understand what data to collect, what to present, and how to incentivize industry to share its data.

> **RECOMMENDATION 2:** The Bureau of Labor Statistics, in collaboration with the Bureau of Economic Analysis and the Census Bureau, should pursue approaches to soliciting input and advice from industry and academia, with a special focus on collaboration with industry. Government statistics require input concerning the data and measures needed, both to ensure the relevancy of concepts being measured and, most importantly, to help government statistics keep up with the rapid pace of change in industry.

DESIGN OF A SATELLITE ACCOUNT (SPECIFICATIONS)

Road Map to a Retail Trade Satellite Account

The panel proposes that the satellite account be based on the concept of a central account with modules for experimentation to address important side questions, data issues, and subjects on which it is difficult coming to a consensus. The first step is to find consensus on a central module that BLS (with the help of BEA and Census) could develop quickly.

One of the first questions to answer is, "What is retail?" Though retail may have a current definition, it is important to consider how it should be defined in the future. These future-oriented ideas may be addressed as modules. Examples of such ideas include digital goods, such as e-books, and the impact of off-shoring. Adapting to the future might require ongoing case studies that involve firms and industry organizations as well as confidential studies of microdata at Federal Statistical Research Data Centers (FSRCDs).

Several existing satellite accounts created by BEA may provide useful models for developing a retail satellite account, given the measurement challenges posed by the retail transformation. The digital economy satellite account includes e-commerce and digital services, which are both important aspects of the retail transformation. The health care satellite account involves a reconceptualization of health care spending, which might suggest novel ways to reflect the changing cost structure of retail. The outdoor recreation satellite account addresses the challenge of dividing up statistics from several industries to combine some of them in a new grouping that is useful to the field. The small business satellite account addresses the challenge of identifying establishments of different sizes, which may also be an important way to divide the data for the retail sector (**Conclusion 4-6**).

The project should begin with aspects of retail that can be defined through a broad consensus, and should then incorporate additions and adaptations as new information becomes available and research is completed.

> **RECOMMENDATION 3:** In implementing a satellite account, the Bureau of Labor Statistics (BLS) and its partners should adopt an iterative and modular approach, starting with feasible options that draw upon the Bureau of Economic Analysis (BEA) industry accounts and the BLS-BEA Integrated Labor Productivity Account to see what insights these might provide about the retail sector and about feasible fixes. The project should provide a set of estimates in a central module, but also a set of submodules to investigate important side questions or alternative measures. It should also outline a set of studies to carry out over time to investigate different questions—assessing importance/relevance, resources required, feasibility, accuracy, need for further research, source data, and benefit versus cost—and suggest possible improvements.

Defining the Retail-Supporting Sector

Of the four options discussed in Chapter 4 for defining retail—distributional, retail-supporting, retail-controlled, and retail enterprise—retail-supporting is closest to what is needed according to the statement of work, and it is the most practical as the basis for a satellite account. The retail-supporting definition will also need to be augmented with retail-supporting auxiliaries (support establishments), as well as with other retail-supporting industries (defined by North American Industry Classification System [NAICS] code) such as computing, intangibles, and leasing (**Conclusion 4-2**).

It is important to start with a relatively simple sector definition to develop expertise and communicate with users. The distributional option was mentioned at the workshop as a possible starting point,[3] but it was viewed as too broad to satisfy the statement of task. Another useful starting point might be to start from the list of NAICS codes to be included in the expanded retail-supporting option, identifying those that are entirely

---

[3] Leonard Nakamura of the Federal Reserve Bank of Philadelphia observed that the distribution sector definition would be welcomed by macroeconomists who seek a streamlined view of the economy.

retail supporting and those that are partly retail supporting. An account that includes only those codes that are entirely retail supporting alongside another account that includes all codes with some retail-supporting activity would together provide lower and upper bounds for what might be gained by a careful development of estimates for splitting the input and output of industries that are partly retail supporting (**Conclusion 4-5**).

> **RECOMMENDATION 4:** The satellite account should cover all retail and retail-supporting establishments, identifying these by combining available information from existing and enhanced data. This group encompasses all establishments supporting the distribution of retail goods to the consumer, excluding the manufacturing and importing of retail goods.

Outputs, Deflation, and Inputs for Measuring Labor Productivity

Chapter 3 reviews existing measures, commenting on their conceptual attributes and the methodological issues surrounding their measurement. Important aspects of conceptual and measurement issues are summarized below.

The three definitions of nominal output considered most appropriate for a study of retail-related industries are gross sales for service-related industries, gross margins for trade-related industries, and value-added for all industries. Gross sales and purchases are measured on the economic survey appropriate to the sector. For trade industries, gross margin is equal to gross sales less purchases (the cost of goods sold). Because purchases are not published for as many detailed NAICS codes in retail trades as are sales, gross margin is similarly available for fewer detailed NAICS codes. Value-added, the purest measure of output, is the most complex to compute, and is more limited in industry detail because it relies on measures of intermediate inputs that are less broadly available (**Conclusion 3-6**).

Nominal output needs to record the changing organization of retail trade and supporting industries and to measure the output of the services it provides, not the value of the goods it sells. Gross sales in service industries and gross margins in trade industries are good measures of industry output, but they produce a misleading double-counted total over all industries. If a consistent total is the goal, the value-added measures of industry output, consistent with GDP, should be used.

Existing price indices provide a way of describing price changes that occur for services and products provided by individual retail outlets. However, these indices do not typically capture the aggregate price changes that result as consumers move from one type of retail outlet to another (**Conclusion 3-7**). The price deflator for retail-sector industries should relate to the change in the *services* the sector provides and to changes in the prices and quality of those services. This differs from price adjustment related to the products the retailer sells, which focus on the characteristics of the goods themselves. Price deflation in the retail-related sector needs to consider, for example, the shifts in services consumers receive when they move from a traditional department store to a warehouse store to e-commerce. Those shifts, in turn, involve changes related to such things as product variety and the process for identifying and obtaining goods (**Conclusion 3-9**).

Real output needs to be measured with a deflator that captures the transformation of the *services* that retail trade provides, including greater variety, efficiency of shopping (ease of price comparisons, quick and low-cost home delivery, etc.), not the increase in productivity coming from the *goods* that retail trade provides. Conceptually, the Producer Price Index (PPI) gross margins deflator is appropriate for deflating gross margins. However, ideally it needs to be adjusted for outlet bias, variety increase, and changes in the services provided by retailers.

While "hours worked" is considered to be the appropriate measure of input for measuring labor productivity, it is improved when work hours are adjusted to reflect the quality of work provided by workers with different skill sets. Current BLS approaches adjust for worker quality by looking at pay differences across groups of workers defined by differences in educational attainment, age, and gender. However, the retail transformation is bringing substantial changes to the workforce with large increases in workers with high-end programming and data analysis skills that support e-commerce. New research in labor economics is investigating ways to measure the skill shifts related to such changes by looking at changes in the tasks involved rather than the educational attainment, age, and gender of the workforce (**Conclusion 3-10**).

Labor input should reflect changes in education and skills accompanying the transformation in retail trade. These issues are key not only to measuring labor productivity but to understanding the impact of the retail trade transformation on productivity, automation, employment, the distribution of income, and the offshoring of jobs. However, additional work is needed to better evaluate the changes in the retail-related labor force and the skills needed.

In summary, there are multiple potential measures of output, deflators, and inputs; some are currently available, whereas others will require future enhancements. The account should be developed with the goal of studying the impact of the different choices.

> **RECOMMENDATION 5:** The satellite account should focus on examining multiple measures of output, deflators, and labor input. Output measures should include gross sales and gross margins for trade industries, gross sales/revenues for other industries, and value-added

for all industries. Deflators should include current margin deflators and new options that capture the changing characteristics of retail trade. Labor input measures should include both simple hours worked and quality-adjusted hours worked to capture the changes in workforce quality. Modules should also be used to evaluate alternative approaches to estimating the split between retail-related and nonretail-related for both output and input.

Potential Experimental Submodules

One of the features of a satellite account with the greatest value is its potential to allow experimentation with alternative concepts and more detailed and alternative definitions. The experimental projects noted in the following are just some of the studies that could be conducted using a satellite account.

Alternative output measures and deflators should be compared in modules. Some of the key decisions to be made in developing a satellite account will be to select output measures, deflators, and input measures. Each of these decisions should be carefully evaluated by incorporating the alternative measures in modules. Hence, for example, there should be modules for comparing output measures: gross sales, gross margins for trade industries, gross sales for service industries, and value-added.

Modules could be used to provide *alternative aggregations, classifications,* and *details of interest* to researchers interested in better understanding productivity, foreign direct investment, and wages. (Examples include data by size of firm, more detailed breakouts by occupation or wages, and foreign-owned versus domestic-owned.) Special attention could be given to apparent divergences between apparently high-productivity big firms and the official statistics for their industries. Modules might also be used to experiment with new measures by making more assumptions or using uncertain data.

Modules could be used to experiment with *quality-adjusted price indexes* that provide a measure of the real output and productivity of retail trade based on the characteristics of today's "transformed" retail trade industry.

A satellite account might incorporate modules to address *products that cross the boundary between goods and services*. It could do this by integrating statistics for related retail products that are now classified in multiple industries, like books, newspapers, movies, and games (which come in physical, audio, and digital form), music (including CDs, digital sales, and streaming), and cars (both sales and leases). The digital economy satellite account might provide a reference.

Modules might be useful for better measuring and allocating *productivity gains* due to various sources, such as imported inputs, domestic IT products sold by retailers, and nonretail-trade support industries, such as transport. Work on extended input-output accounts and global value chains at the United Nations, Organisation for Economic Co-operation and Development (OECD), and other international and national statistical agencies, including BEA, could be helpful in understanding the role of international trade and investment in measuring the source of productivity chains.

An account that could capture the *many services provided by today's retail trade firms and the firms that support them* would be invaluable. These services include the broad diversity of products available at one site/location; the ability to compare prices and product characteristics; and rapid and low-cost home delivery. A satellite account could incorporate estimates of consumer shopping time that would allow an integrated analysis of the labor productivity implications of the increased shopping and delivery options being provided by many retailers.

Modules that help to assess and illuminate the *accuracy and utility of employment and productivity data* could be used to both update and identify needed improvements to these data through new research, new methods, and new source data. For example, new source data might include NETS, NPD, and credit card information. NPD and credit card data could potentially provide high-frequency data related to sales revenues and purchases to help prepare more timely estimates.

RECOMMENDATION 6: Experimental submodules may address more specialized issues that contribute to the transition in retail trade, such as (1) international trade and global value chains; (2) digitization; (3) labor quality; and (4) providing real-time and subsector analyses. Over time, the central module would incorporate improvements developed in the submodules and in new data collection.

STUDYING AND SOLVING DATA ISSUES

Identifying and filling data gaps, correcting for errors in data, using data to help define the scope of the retail-related sector, and exploring the use of new data sources will be a major part of the effort to design and build a retail-related satellite account. There are data gaps and data issues associated with the Census Bureau's economic surveys, with the BLS employment surveys, and some errors in productivity result from the use of separate business registers by BLS and Census. On a more forward-looking note, a study using microdata at the Census Bureau could help define the scope of the project, and identifying and using alternative new data sources might help improve timeliness and detail. These data sources are primarily discussed in Chapter 3 and are summarized below.

While these are the key issues identified by the panel, they are not the only data deficiencies that will be identified during the construction of a retail-related satellite account. Identifying data gaps and data needs and working to improve accuracy when the data are deficient will become a major effort going forward. Improved source data are needed to make substantive progress on measuring the transformation of retail trade.

Data Gaps for Output-Related Data (Census Bureau)

The data available from the Census Bureau's Economic Census and surveys are the foundation of U.S. economic statistics. However, data available for retail-trade-related industries are less extensive than information collected for other industries and significantly less extensive than the data available for manufacturing. Given that retail trade has become a key driver of the economy, it would be prudent to expand on the data available to measure the retail-related sector more accurately. Examples of deficiencies include the following.

- *Purchase data* are needed to compute gross margins, but the only purchase data for retail are collected in the Annual Retail Trade Survey (ARTS), not in the Economic Census. As a result, purchase data are not available at the establishment level for retail establishments, and benchmarking to the Economic Census requires assumptions that likely affect the quality of estimated gross margins.
- *Product detail for retail sales* is not covered by ARTS, though it is covered in the Economic Census of retail trade. ARTS does not request any industry breakdown of sales activity, and it offers no information on gross margins by product class. However, these missing data are needed to accurately and separately allocate sales and purchases to codes. This lack of detail may affect the quality of estimated gross margins. Changes in measured gross margins in ARTS likely reflect compositional changes in product mix that are impossible to detect under the current system.
- *Data on operating expenses* are needed to compute value-added. Operating expenses for retail and wholesale trade establishments are collected as an aggregate of an enterprise's establishments on ARTS[4] and the Annual Wholesale Trade Survey (AWTS) once every 5 years during Economic Census years. Data on expenses are not collected at the establishment level on the Economic Census.
- *Auxiliaries* are a key concept for quantifying the impact of vertical integration in a retail-related satellite account. Although some data are available from the Economic Census, there are limited ways to estimate the value an auxiliary provides to its enterprise.

---

[4] See https://www.census.gov/programs-surveys/economic-census/data/bes.html.

In addition, BLS currently has limited information to designate auxiliaries (**Conclusion 3-4**).

Including new questions in ARTS and in the retail trade census could result in better integration between ARTS (which provides gross margins and operating expenses at the enterprise level with little industry/product detail) and the retail trade census (which provides industry/product detail of sales at the establishment level). However, this is only a feasible solution if survey reporting entities have access to the needed data so they can report it. The panel understands that this is a key data issue. There may be administrative data from IRS that could address expense data gaps, if they were available for statistical uses within the federal government. Identifying solutions to data gap issues is important to making sure government statistics evolve to measure a changing industry. An interagency team led by BLS and including representatives from BEA, Census, and potentially IRS could identify critical data gaps and address solutions. Collaboration with industry could help to ensure that industry could provide the requested new information without an undue burden.

Data Gaps for Employment (BLS)—Splitting Input

The statement of task asks for ways to identify the proportion of output, employment, and hours outside of retail trade that are directed toward supporting retail trade. Options are available for splitting retail-related outputs. For output this can be achieved initially by building upon and disaggregating elements of the BLS-BEA integrated industry-level production account, BEA industry accounts, and detailed Census Bureau survey data. Approaches that use existing data on commodities transported are also likely to be useful (**Conclusion 4-4**).

The employment side of this project is very important. There are many questions about the net impact of e-commerce on jobs and employment. Estimating how many people are working in retail and retail-supporting industries, as well as the net change in jobs and pay, would be very helpful by itself as well as useful for measuring productivity (**Conclusion 4-2**).

Solving the problem of splitting hours worked in retail-related industries will likely require new methods, creative use of alternative data sources, and potentially augmenting existing surveys. Some approaches proposed during the workshop included evaluating data that might be available from trade associations and identifying data items that companies might be able to report, such as the commodity employees worked with (e.g., handling aircraft engines versus clothing).

Business Registers/Classification

Labor productivity is measured as the ratio of change in output divided by change in input. Nominal output is measured through Census Bureau surveys. Labor input and price deflators are measured through BLS surveys. The two agencies use separate business registers with separate classifications of business establishments by NAICS code as sampling frames for their surveys. The resulting differences in statistics produced by the two agencies likely contribute to errors in the estimation of productivity, because different establishments may contribute to the numerator and denominator. This error most likely has a time-varying component, because each agency also updates its business lists on a different schedule (**Conclusion 3-2**).

The challenges concerning the use of multiple business registers by the U.S. statistical system has been a topic of concern for years, with solutions recommended in reports by the National Academies of Sciences, Engineering, and Medicine. This panel proposes a multistep process to address this issue, although some steps/projects can be addressed simultaneously because they involve different groups of people. The process might include the following:

Shorter-term efforts would focus on specific projects to support the development of a satellite account for retail. For example, a detailed evaluation of linked microdata at an FSRDC could be targeted toward developing adjustment factors to account for differences in concept between output and input in the retail-related satellite account (**Conclusion 3-4**).

BLS annually receives a file containing Census Bureau Firm IDs, employer identity numbers (EINs), and establishment detail. However, BLS does not use the Census file on a regular basis, because the reconciliation of EINs between Census and BLS is labor-intensive and time-consuming. It would be beneficial to be able to quantify all of the activity under firm IDs that have some establishments classified as retail and for which linking BLS and Census firm and establishment data might help in identifying retail-related auxiliaries in BLS data, for example, something that is not currently possible. This has the potential for helping in the development of a satellite on retail-trade-supporting activities (**Conclusion 3-3**).

The ideal long-term solution to the issue of separate business registers being developed, maintained, and used by BLS, BEA, and Census would be to remove the obstacles to data sharing noted in the National Academies (NASEM, 2017) and National Research Council (2007) reports and for the federal government to develop and use a single, common business register (**Conclusion 3-5**).

RECOMMENDATION 7: Measures should be taken immediately to facilitate the expansion of the Confidential Information Protection and

Statistical Efficiency Act to increase the kinds of information that may be shared among statistical agencies for the purpose of reconciling the business lists and for the design of special surveys. This expansion of data sharing can be accomplished by (1) Congress acting to enact legislation that revises the Internal Revenue Service (IRS) Code Section 6103(j) to extend authorized access to IRS tax information to the Bureau of Economic Analysis and Bureau of Labor Statistics; (2) the Treasury Department initiating an update of the IRS regulations that clarify purpose and detail specific items that can be shared with authorized agencies; or (3) a combination of the preceding two activities[5] (National Research Council, 2007, p. 111, Recommendation 15).

The panel is hopeful that these legislative hurdles to development of a single business register may be resolved. The semi-final step would be the actual development and maintenance of a single consolidated business register for use by BLS, BEA, and the Census Bureau. A longer-term goal is a business register that could also be used as a sampling frame by other government agencies. This would be a significant undertaking and might require resolving additional legal issues. In addition, it would require addressing operational issues, such as coordinating survey feedback when two (or more) organizations use the same business register; agreeing on the classification of establishments; agreeing on the linkage between establishments, including auxiliaries, and their enterprise; and identifying roles and responsibilities, such as keeping structures up-to-date and approving changes. Maintaining a common business register would mean that BLS, BEA, the Census Bureau, and IRS would have to work together very closely to ensure coherence.

RECOMMENDATION 8: The Bureau of Labor Statistics, Bureau of Economic Analysis, Census Bureau, and Internal Revenue Service should establish an interagency task force, potentially including other relevant agencies, to develop a plan for implementing a single consolidated business register to use as the sample frame for all business surveys. The task force should scope out the problem and identify what needs to be done and what is required to get it done.

Better Defining the Retail-Related Sector

To better understand the changes in retail-related industries, a collaborative effort between BLS, BEA, and Census Bureau staff could make use

---

[5]Changes in access to tax data are required for BEA and BLS, not because BEA or BLS needs direct access to tax data, but because the Census business register is built on IRS data and some of the Census data directly use tax data or are considered to be "comingled" with tax data.

of microdata as a laboratory to better understand many of the complicated aspects of developing a retail-related satellite account. The purpose would be to use the concepts and data to gain a better understanding of key issues, such as assessing the structural changes associated with the retail trade transformation by size of enterprise and understanding the role of auxiliaries and other nonretail establishments within retail trade enterprises (**Conclusion 4-3**).

Data Gaps for Timeliness and Detail

As described in Chapter 3, examples of private-sector data sources include proprietary/commercial data, web-scraped data, data from trade associations or other private groups, data from credit card companies or banks, data from individual stores or loyalty programs, and so on. Typical challenges with proprietary data include inadequate representation, lack of documentation, and challenging nondisclosure agreements.

Private-sector data such as scanner data might support capturing both quantities and prices of purchases to estimate the price effects of consumers moving between retail outlets (**Conclusion 3-10**). Additionally, private-sector, credit card and payroll processing data have been used to provide more timely information about economic output, prices, and input that could potentially be used to provide more timely estimates for labor productivity in the retail-related sector (**Conclusion 3-12**). One key challenge in using private-sector data is understanding how well they represent all businesses, both large and small. For all their challenges, private-sector data have some key advantages, including timeliness and detail.

RECOMMENDATION 9: Developing a retail-related satellite account will require considerable effort to acquire and use data and to address data gaps in existing data. The panel has identified the following data issues that need to be addressed, but others will arise during the course of the study. Individual projects include: Filling data gaps in the Economic Census and Annual Economic Surveys that relate to the calculation of gross margins, value added, and the contribution of auxiliaries; identifying data to estimate the split in hours worked between retail-related and nonretail-related for retail-related service industries; correcting for differences in numerator and denominator of productivity caused by the use of different business registers and classifications; and exploring the use of private-sector data—such as scanner data, bankcard data, and payroll processing data—to improve the timeliness and detail provided in the account. Some of these efforts are best accomplished by a team that is granted access to the Census Bureau's economic microdata from the business register and from its Economic Census and to surveys at a Federal Statistical Research Data Center.

References

Acemoglu, D., and Autor, D.H. (2011). Skills, tasks, and technologies: Implications for employment and earnings. In O. Ashenfelter and D. Card (Eds.), *Handbook of Labor Economics* (volume 4b, pp. 1043-1171). Amsterdam, the Netherlands: Elsevier/North Holland.

Acemoglu, D., and Restrepo, P. (2018). The race between man and machine: Implications of technology for growth, factor shares, and employment. *American Economic Review 108*(6): 1488-1542.

Aghion, P., Bergeaud, A., Boppart, T., Klenow, P.J., and Li, H. (2019). Missing growth from creative destruction. *American Economic Review 109*(8): 2795-2822.

Aladangady, A., Aron-Dine, S., Dunn, W., Feiveson, L., Lengermann, P., and Sahm C. (2019). *From Transactions Data to Economic Statistics: Constructing Real-time, High-frequency, Geographic Measures of Consumer Spending*. Finance and Economics Discussion Series 2019-057. Washington, DC: Divisions of Research & Statistics and Monetary Affairs, Federal Reserve Board. Available: https://www.federalreserve.gov/econres/feds/files/2019057pap.pdf.

Autor, D.H. (2013). The 'Task approach' to labor markets: An overview. *Journal of Labour Market Research 46*(3). doi: 10.1007/s12651-013-0128-z.

Becker, R., Elvery, J., Foster, L., Krizan, C.J., Nguyen, S., and Talan, D. (2005). *A Comparison of the Business Registers Used by the Bureau of Labor Statistics and the Bureau of the Census*. Available: https://www.bls.gov/osmr/research-papers/2005/pdf/st050270.pdf.

Berndt, E.R., Griliches, Z., and Rappaport, N.J. (1995). Econometric estimates of price indexes for personal computers in the 1990's. *Journal of Econometrics 68*: 243-268.

Bureau of Labor Statistics (BLS). (2020). *CNSTAT Consensus Panel on Measuring the Transformation of Retail Trade and Related Activities: Summary of Issues*. Background paper prepared for the panel by the Bureau of Labor Statistics.

Cajner, T., Crane, L., Decker, R., Hamins-Puertolas, A., Kurz, C., and Radler, T. (2018). *Using Payroll Processor Microdata to Measure Aggregate Labor Market Activity*. Finance and Economics Discussion Series 2018-005. Washington, DC: Divisions of Research & Statistics and Monetary Affairs, Federal Reserve Board.

Cavallo, A., and Rigobon, R. (2016). The billion prices project: Using online prices for measurement and research. *Journal of Economic Perspectives 30*(2): 151-178.

Cole, R., Chen, Y.C., Barquin-Stolleman, J., Dulberger, E., Helvacian, N., and Hodge J.H. (1986). Quality adjusted price indexes for computer processors and selected peripheral equipment. *Survey of Current Business* (January): 41-50.

Diewert, E.W., and Feenstra, R.C. (2019). *Estimating the Benefits of New Products*. NBER Working Paper 25991. Cambridge, MA: National Bureau of Economic Research. Available: https://www.nber.org/papers/w25991.

Ding, X., Fort, T., Redding, S., and Schott, P. (2020). *Structural Change Within Versus Across Firms: Evidence from the United States*. Working Paper. Available: http://faculty.tuck.dartmouth.edu/teresa-fort/research.

Eldridge, L., Garner, C., Howells, T, Moyer, B., Russell, M., Samuels, J., Strassner, E., and Wasshausen, D. (2020). Toward a BEA-BLS integrated industry-level production account for 1947-2016. Chapter 11 (pp. 221-249) in *Measuring Economic Growth and Productivity: Foundations, KLEMS Production Models, and Extensions*, edited by Barbara Fraumeni. Academics Press. Available: https://www.sciencedirect.com/science/article/pii/B9780128175965000111.

Fairman, K., Foster, L., Krizan, C.J., and Rucker, I. (2008). *An Analysis of Key Differences in Micro Data: Results from the Business List Comparison Project*. Available: https://www.bls.gov/osmr/research-papers/2008/st080020.htm.

Farrell, D., and Grieg, F. (2015). *Weathering Volatility: Big Data on the Financial Ups and Downs of U.S. Individuals*. JPMorgan Chase & Co. Institute. Available: https://www.jpmorganchase.com/content/dam/jpmc/jpmorgan-chase-and-co/institute/pdf/54918-jpmc-institute-report-2015-aw5.pdf.

Feenstra, R.C. (1994). New product varieties and the measurement of international prices. *American Economic Review 84*(1): 157-177.

Fixler, D., and Landefeld, S. (2006). The importance of data sharing to consistent macroeconomic statistics. In National Research Council, *Improving Business Statistics through Interagency Data Sharing: Summary of a Workshop*. Washington, DC: The National Academies Press. Available: https://doi.org/10.17226/11738.

Fort, T., and Klimek, S. (2018). *The Effects of Industry Classification Changes on U.S. Employment Composition*. Washington, DC: Center for Economic Studies, U.S. Census Bureau. Available: https://www2.census.gov/ces/wp/2018/CES-WP-18-28.pdf.

Foster, L., Haltiwanger, J., Klimek, S., Krizan, C.J., and Ohlmacher, S. (2016). The evolution of national retail chains: How we got here. In E. Basker (Ed.), *Handbook on the Economics of Retailing and Distribution* (Chapter 1). Cheltenham, UK: Edward Elgar. Available: https://www.elgaronline.com/view/edcoll/9781783477371/9781783477371.00009.xml.

Gollop, F.M., Fraumeni, B., and Jorgenson, D. (1987). *Productivity and U.S. Economic Growth*. Cambridge, MA: Harvard University Press.

Hatzius, J. (2017). *US Daily: The Internet and Inflation: How Big Is the Amazon Effect?* Goldman Sachs Economic Research, August 2.

Highfill, T., Cao, R., Schwinn, R., Prisinzano, R., and Leung, D. (March 2020). *Measuring the Small Business Economy*. BEA Working Paper Series, WP2020-4. Washington, DC: Bureau of Economic Analysis. Available: https://www.bea.gov/system/files/papers/BEA-WP2020-4_0.pdf.

Horrigan, M. (2013). *Big Data: A Perspective from the BLS*. Available: https://magazine.amstat.org/blog/2013/01/01/sci-policy-jan2013/.

Hortaçsu, A., and Syverson, C. (2015). The ongoing evolution of U.S. retail: A format tug-of-war. *Journal of Economic Perspectives 29*(4): 89-112. Available: https://www.aeaweb.org/articles?id=10.1257/jep.29.4.89.

ILO/IMF/OECD/UNECE/Eurostat/The World Bank. (2004). *Consumer Price Index Manual: Theory and Practice*. Geneva: ILO Publications.

Jorgenson, D., and Griliches, Z. (1967*)*. The explanation of productivity change. *Review of Economic Studies 34*(3): 249-283.

Jorgenson, D., Ho, M., and Samuels, J. (2016). *Education, Participation, and the Revival of U.S. Economic Growth*. Working Paper 22453. Cambridge, MA: National Bureau of Economic Research. Available: http://www.nber.org/papers/w22453.

Lafontaine, F., and Sivadasan, J. (forthcoming). The recent evolution of physical retail markets: Online retailing, big box stores, and the rise of restaurants. In A. Chatterji, J. Lerner, S. Stern, and M.J. Andrews (Eds.), *The Role of Innovation and Entrepreneurship in Economic Growth*. NBER conference held January 7-8, 2020. Chicago: University of Chicago Press.

Mandel, M. (2017). *How Ecommerce Creates Jobs and Reduces Income Inequality*. Washington: DC: Progressive Policy Institute. Available: https://www.progressivepolicy.org/wp-content/uploads/2017/09/PPI_ECommerceInequality_2017.pdf.

Manser, M.E. (2005). Productivity measures for retail trade: Data and issues. *Monthly Labor Review* (July): 30-38.

Mian, A., Rao, K., and Sufi, A. (2013). Household balance sheets, consumption, and the economic slump. *Quarterly Journal of Economics 128*(4): 1687-1726.

Moulton, B.R. (2018). *The Measurement of Output, Prices, and Productivity: What's Changed Since the Boskin Commission?* Washington, DC: The Brookings Institution. Available: https://www.brookings.edu/wp-content/uploads/2018/07/Moulton-report-v2.pdf.

Nakamura, A.O., Diewert, W.E., Greenlees, J.S., Nakamura, L.I., and Reinsdorf, M.B. (2015). Sourcing substitution and related price index biases. In S.N. Houseman and M. Mandel (Eds.), *Measuring Globalization: Better Trade Statistics for Better Policy, Volume 1, Biases to Price, Output, and Productivity Statistics from Trade* (pp. 21-88). Kalamazoo, MI: W.E. Upjohn Institute for Employment Research. doi: 10.17848/9780880994903.vol1ch2.

National Academies of Sciences, Engineering, and Medicine (NASEM). (2017). *Innovations in Federal Statistics: Combining Data Sources While Protecting Privacy*. Washington, DC: The National Academies Press. Available: https://doi.org/10.17226/24652.

NASEM. (2020). *A Consumer Food Data System for 2030 and Beyond*. Washington, DC: The National Academies Press. Available: https://doi.org/10.17226/25657.

National Research Council (NRC). (2007). *Understanding Business Dynamics: An Integrated Data System for America's Future*. J. Haltiwanger, L.M. Lynch, and C. Mackie (Eds.). Panel on Measuring Business Formation, Dynamics, and Performance; Committee on National Statistics; Division of Behavioral and Social Sciences and Education. Washington, DC: The National Academies Press.

Neiman, B., and Vavra, J.S. (2019). *The Rise of Niche Consumption*. Working Paper 26134. Cambridge, MA: National Bureau of Economic Research. Available: http://www.nber.org/papers/w26134.

Redding, S.J., and Weinstein, D.E. (2016). *A Unified Approach to Estimating Demand and Welfare*. Working Paper 22479. Cambridge, MA: National Bureau of Economic Research. Available: https://www.nber.org/system/files/working_papers/w22479/revisions/w22479.rev1.pdf.

Reinsdorf, M. (1993). The effect of outlet price differentials on the U.S. consumer price index. In *Price Measurements and Their Uses*, edited by M. Foss, M. Manser, and A. Young. NBER Studies in Income and Wealth 57. Chicago: University of Chicago Press.

Reinsdorf, M., and Slaughter, M.J., editors. (2009). Introduction in *International Trade in Services and Intangibles in the Era of Globalization*. NBER Book Series Studies in Income and Wealth. Chicago: University of Chicago Press. Available: https://www.nber.org/books/rein09-1/.

Smith, D. (2019). *Concentration and Foreign Sourcing in the U.S. Retail Sector.* 2019 meeting papers 1258, Society for Economic Dynamics. Available: https://ideas.repec.org/p/red/sed019/1258.html.

Smith, P. (2020). *Satellite Accounting in Canada.* Prepared for Workshop on Measuring the Transformation in Retail Trade, June 22-23, 2020. Available: https://www150.statcan.gc.ca/n1/pub/13-605-x/2020001/article/00002-eng.htm or https://www.nationalacademies.org/event/06-22-2020/measuring-the-transformation-of-retail-trade-and-related-activities-public-workshop.

Triplett, J., and Bosworth, B. (2004). *Productivity in the U.S. Services Sector: New Sources of Economic Growth.* Washington, DC: Brookings Institution Press.

U.S. Department of the Treasury. (2014). *General Explanations of the Administration's Fiscal Year 2015 Revenue Proposals.* Available: https://www.treasury.gov/resourcecenter/tax-policy/Documents/General-Explanations-FY2015.pdf.

U.S. Office of Management and Budget. (2016). Chapter 7: Building the capacity to produce and use evidence. In *Analytical Perspectives: Budget of the United States Government: Fiscal Year 2017* (pp. 69-77). Washington, DC: Government Printing Office. Available: https://obamawhitehouse.archives.gov/sites/default/fles/omb/budget/fy2017/assets/ap_7_evidence.pdf.

Appendix A

Agenda for the Panel's Workshop

Consensus Panel Study on Measuring the Transformation of
Retail Trade and Related Activities

Meeting 2: June 22-23, 2020

Virtual workshop to discuss the transformation,
data challenges, and potential solutions

Monday, June 22, 2020

10:00-10:25 Welcome and Overview of the Workshop
    10:00-10:05 Welcome, **Brian Harris-Kojetin**, director, CNSTAT
    10:05-10:10 Welcome, **Lucy Eldridge**, BLS
    10:10-10:25 Workshop overview, **J. Steven Landefeld**, panel chair

What Is Retail and How Is It Changing?

10:25-11:25 Research on Retail Changes. Moderator: **Gregory Duncan**, panel member
    10:25-10:45 Statements by participants. **Emek Basker**, US Census Bureau; **Chad Syverson**, University of Chicago; and **Steve Noble**, McKinsey
    10:45-11:05 Panel discussion
    11:05-11:25 Discussion

11:25-11:40 Break

11:40-12:50 Industry Perspectives of Industry Changes: Past, Present, Future Moderator: **Jack Kleinhenz**, Retail Trade Federation
   11:40-11:45 Overview: **Jack Kleinhenz**, Retail Trade Federation
   11:45-12:05 Statements by panelists. **Drew Spata**, Macy's; **David Glick**, FLEXE (formerly Amazon); **Richard Phillips**, Yale Divinity School (former chairman and former CEO of Pilot Freight Services); **Anne Goodchild**, University of Washington
   12:05-12:25 Panel discussion
   12:25-12:50 Discussion

12:50-2:00 Lunch break

Key Measurement and Data Challenges

2:00-4:00 Data: Availability, Needs, Discrepancies, and Gaps. A panel discussion. Moderator: **Wesley Yung**, panel member
   2:00-2:35 Initial statement by panelists. Panelists: **Ken Robertson**, BLS; **Jon D. Samuels**, BEA; **Matthew Russell**, BLS; **Leland Crane**, Federal Reserve; **Ian Thomas**, Census Bureau; **Edward Watkins**, Census Bureau
   2:35-3:15 Panel discussion
   3:15-3:30 Break
   3:30-4:00 Discussion

4:00 Adjourn

Tuesday, June 23, 2020

Potential Improvements to Measuring Employment and Productivity in Retail-related Sectors

10:00-11:30 Towards a BLS Satellite Account for Retail: Moderator: **Carol Corrado**, panel member
   10:00-11:00 Panel discussion. Panelists: **Brian Chansky**, BLS; **Tina Highfill**, BEA; **Philip Smith**, Statistics Canada (retired); **Marshall Reinsdorf**, International Monetary Fund
   11:00-11:10 Discussant: **Leonard Nakamura**, panel member
   11:10-11:30 Discussion

11:30-11:45 Break

11:45-12:30　Quality-adjusted Prices for Retail. Moderator: **Dale Jorgensen,** panel member
  11:45-12:00　**Ana Aizcorbe,** BEA
  12:00-12:15　**Brendan Williams** and **Bonnie Murphy,** BLS
  12:15-12:30　Discussion

12:30-2:00　Lunch break

2:00-3:00　Uses of Bottom-Up in Measuring Employment and Productivity. Moderator: **Kelly McConville,** panel member
  2:00-2:30　**Teresa Fort** and **John Haltiwanger,** panel members
  2:30-3:00　Discussion

3:00-3:20　Break

3:20-4:20　Global Value Chains. Moderator: **Michael Mandel,** panel member
  3:20-3:40　**Dominic Smith,** BLS
  3:40-4:00　**Robert Feenstra,** UC Davis
  4:00-4:20　Discussion

4:20　Adjourn

Appendix B

Retail Output, Hours, and Labor Productivity, 1997-2018

Industry	Measure	Year 1997	Year 2007	Year 2018	Index Change 1997-2018	Productivity Change 1997-2018 Total	Productivity Change 1997-2018 Annual	Productivity Change Total 1997-2007	Productivity Change Total 2007-2018	Productivity Change Annual 1997-2007	Productivity Change Annual 2007-2018
44,45 - Retail trade	Sales	64.916	100.000	124.940	92.5%	89.0%	3.1%	50.9%	25.2%	4.2%	2.1%
	Margin	75.329	103.21	125.78	67.0%	64.0%	2.4%	34.3%	22.1%	3.0%	1.8%
	Value Added	76.897	105.14	120.33	56.5%	53.7%	2.1%	34.0%	14.7%	3.0%	1.3%
	Hours	97.987	100.000	99.785	1.8%						
441 - Motor vehicle and parts dealers	Sales	70.863	100.000	120.501	70.0%	52.6%	2.0%	32.9%	14.8%	2.9%	1.3%
	Margin	101.77	104.82	155	52.3%	36.6%	1.5%	-3.0%	40.9%	-0.3%	3.2%
	Value Added	95.839	109.44	151.98	58.6%	42.3%	1.7%	7.5%	32.3%	0.7%	2.6%
	Hours	94.166	100.000	104.962	11.5%						
444 - Building material and garden supply stores	Sales	61.031	100.000	110.475	81.0%	68.8%	2.5%	34.9%	25.1%	3.0%	2.1%
	Margin	76.671	115.58	121.92	59.0%	48.3%	1.9%	24.1%	19.5%	2.2%	1.6%
	Value Added	67.394	108.69	109.26	62.1%	51.2%	2.0%	32.8%	13.9%	2.9%	1.2%
	Hours	82.319	100.000	88.284	7.2%						
445 - Food and beverage stores	Sales	94.752	100.000	114.421	20.8%	34.0%	1.4%	21.6%	10.2%	2.0%	0.9%
	Margin	100.54	104.41	102.22	1.7%	12.9%	0.6%	19.6%	-5.7%	1.8%	-0.5%
	Value Added	120.6	112.74	95.773	-20.6%	-11.9%	-0.6%	7.7%	-18.2%	0.7%	-1.8%
	Hours	115.207	100.000	103.795	-9.9%						
446 - Health and personal care stores	Sales	62.581	100.000	108.074	72.7%	39.1%	1.6%	37.4%	1.2%	3.2%	0.1%
	Margin	76.623	93.07	117.96	53.9%	24.0%	1.0%	4.4%	18.7%	0.4%	1.6%
	Value Added	92.852	95.913	116.56	25.5%	1.1%	0.1%	-11.2%	13.8%	-1.2%	1.2%
	Hours	85.972	100.000	106.769	24.2%						
447 - Gasoline stations	Sales	89.167	100.000	102.647	15.1%	26.0%	1.1%	29.4%	-2.6%	2.6%	-0.2%
	Margin	100.86	108.93	98.78	-2.1%	7.2%	0.3%	24.6%	-14.0%	2.2%	-1.4%
	Value Added	132.34	130.25	74.198	-43.9%	-38.6%	-2.3%	13.5%	-46.0%	1.3%	-5.4%
	Hours	115.357	100.000	105.401	-8.6%						
448 - Clothing and clothing accessories stores	Sales	55.427	100.000	116.855	110.8%	118.6%	3.8%	73.4%	26.1%	5.7%	2.1%
	Margin	59.241	103.56	114.14	92.7%	99.8%	3.4%	68.0%	18.9%	5.3%	1.6%
	Value Added	69.112	106.33	113.8	64.7%	70.8%	2.6%	47.8%	15.5%	4.0%	1.3%
	Hours	96.087	100.000	92.657	-3.6%						
452 - General merchandise stores	Sales	54.865	100.000	121.999	122.4%	76.7%	2.7%	52.2%	16.1%	4.3%	1.4%
	Margin	61.229	108.4	114.25	86.6%	48.3%	1.9%	47.8%	0.3%	4.0%	0.0%
	Value Added	61.185	112.98	119.22	94.9%	54.9%	2.1%	54.2%	0.4%	4.4%	0.0%
	Hours	83.509	100.000	105.060	25.8%						
454 - Nonstore retailers	Sales	34.660	100.000	231.360	567.5%	482.3%	8.8%	198.2%	95.3%	11.5%	6.3%
	Margin	41.42	81.045	177.01	327.3%	272.8%	6.5%	102.2%	84.3%	7.3%	5.7%
	Value Added	34.5	72.103	159.62	362.7%	303.6%	6.9%	116.0%	86.8%	8.0%	5.8%
	Hours	103.360	100.000	118.494	14.6%						
42 - Wholesale trade	Sales	66.058	100.000	109.230	65.4%	66.5%	2.5%	49.4%	11.4%	4.1%	1.0%
	Margin	57.984	88.297	114.24	97.0%	98.3%	3.3%	50.2%	32.0%	4.2%	2.6%
	Value Added	68.023	102.07	113.09	66.3%	67.4%	2.5%	48.0%	13.0%	4.0%	1.1%
	Hours	98.660	100.000	98.009	-0.7%						
493 - Warehousing and storage	Sales	60.027	100.000	156.161	160.2%	0.7%	0.0%	15.2%	-12.5%	1.4%	-1.2%
	Margin	28.37	62.763	119.72	322.0%	63.4%	2.4%	52.9%	6.9%	4.3%	0.6%
	Value Added	48.383	80.867	144.62	198.9%	15.8%	0.7%	15.5%	0.2%	1.5%	0.0%
	Hours worked	69.125	100.000	178.501	158.2%						

SOURCES: Output measured by sales revenue ("Sales") from U.S. Bureau of Labor Statistics (BLS), Division of Industry Productivity Studies (https://www.bls.gov/lpc/lpc_by_industry_and_measure.xlsx using the "Output" field). Output measured by gross margin ("Margin") and value added ("Value Added") from U.S. Bureau of Economic Analysis, Industry Data webpage (using the "Chain-Type Quantity Index" for both gross output and value added). Hours data ("Hours") from BLS (https://www.bls.gov/lpc/lpc_by_industry_and_measure.xlsx using the "Hours" field). All four series described using indices where 2007=100 (Sales, Hours) or 2012=100 (Margin, Value Added). Labor productivity calculated by dividing change in output by change in hours worked, using hours data.

Appendix C

Biographical Sketches of Panel Members

J. STEVEN LANDEFELD (*Chair*) was director of the U.S. Bureau of Economic Analysis (BEA) for nearly 20 years. Since his retirement, Landefeld has served as a distinguished visiting professor at the U.S. Naval Academy and as an adviser and consultant to various organizations, including the United Nations, the Committee on National Statistics, and BEA. His current research focuses on the development of "satellite" accounts that better measure economic well-being by measuring the distribution of production and income, the sustainability of growth, and auxiliary accounts on topics such globalization, energy, the environment, health, human capital, and household production. As director of BEA, he led the Bureau in a number of measurement improvements including regular updates using new methodologies and source data to provide more timely and relevant data. He is a recipient of the President's Distinguished Executive Award, the National Association for Business Economics and American Statistical Association joint Julius Shiskin Award, and other national and international awards. He has regularly published works on economic measurement throughout his career. He has B.A., M.A., and Ph.D. degrees in economics, all from the University of Maryland, College Park.

CAROL A. CORRADO is research director at the Conference Board in Washington, DC. She also works with the Conference Board's China Center for Research on Economics and Business. Corrado is a member of the executive committee of the National Bureau of Economic Research's (NBER's) Conference on Research on Income and Wealth and is an organizer of a workshop on economic measurement at the NBER's annual Summer

Institute. She has authored key papers on the macroeconomic analysis of intangible investment and capital, including the winner of the International Association of Research on Income and Wealth's 2010 Kendrick Prize and a paper in the NBER volume on *Measuring Capital in the New Economy*. Corrado received the American Statistical Association's prestigious Julius Shiskin Award for Economic Statistics in 2003 in recognition of her leadership in these areas and was a recipient of a Special Achievement Award from the Board of Governors of the Federal Reserve System in 1998. She has a B.S. degree in management science from Carnegie Mellon University, and a Ph.D. in economics from the University of Pennsylvania.

GREGORY DUNCAN is senior principal economist, technologist, and machine learning scientist at Amazon and affiliate professor of economics at the University of Washington. At Amazon, he has worked on addressing numerous econometric and statistical issues throughout the company, including projects related to policy and competition, forecasting, the use of machine learning, and supply chain research. He is also a co-founder of the Amazon Machine Learning University. He has a B.A. degree in economics from the University of Washington, and an M.A. degree in statistics and a Ph.D. in economics, both from the University of California, Berkeley.

TERESA C. FORT is an associate professor of business administration at the Tuck School of Business at Dartmouth College. She conducts research in international trade and industrial organization. Her current work analyzes how technology affects firm-level offshoring and production fragmentation decisions, and the impact of these decisions on domestic employment and innovation. Fort is a faculty research fellow at the National Bureau of Economic Research and a research affiliate at the Centre for Economic Policy Research. She holds a Ph.D. in economics from the University of Maryland, and a B.A. degree from the University of Virginia.

JOHN C. HALTIWANGER is a distinguished university professor in the Department of Economics at the University of Maryland, College Park. He also serves as research associate at the National Bureau of Economic Research, senior research fellow at the Center for Economic Studies at the U.S. Census Bureau, and fellow of the Society of Labor Economics and the Econometric Society. His research increasingly uses the data and measures on firm dynamics from a substantial number of advanced, emerging, and transition economies. Haltiwanger has published more than 100 academic articles and numerous books, including *Job Creation and Destruction*. He has a Sc.B. in applied mathematics-economics from Brown University and a Ph.D. in economics from the Johns Hopkins University.

DALE W. JORGENSON is the Samuel W. Morris university professor in the Department of Economics at Harvard University. Jorgenson was awarded the John Bates Clark Medal by the American Economic Association and served as its president in 2000. He was a founding member of the Board on Science, Technology, and Economic Policy of the National Research Council and served as its chair. Jorgenson has conducted groundbreaking research on information technology and economic growth, energy and the environment, tax policy and investment behavior, and applied econometrics. He is the author of more than 300 articles on economics and the author and editor of 37 books. He has a B.A. degree in economics from Reed College and a Ph.D. in economics from Harvard.

MICHAEL MANDEL is chief economic strategist at the Progressive Policy Institute in Washington, DC, senior fellow at Wharton's Mack Institute for Innovation Management at the University of Pennsylvania, and fellow at the Manufacturing Policy Initiative at Indiana University. With experience spanning policy, academics, and business, Mandel has helped lead the public conversation about the economic and business impact of technology for the past two decades. He taught at New York University's Stern School of Business and his introductory economics textbook, *Economics: The Basics*, is currently in its fourth edition. Mandel holds an A.B. in applied mathematics and a Ph.D. in economics from Harvard.

KELLY MCCONVILLE is assistant professor of statistics at Reed College, specializing in survey sampling. In her work, she develops survey estimation techniques that combine data collected under a complex sampling design with auxiliary data sources. McConville has collaborated with the U.S. Forest Service's Forest Inventory and Analysis Program and the U.S. Bureau of Labor Statistics. She co-chairs two national programs: the Undergraduate Statistics Project Competition and the Electronic Undergraduate Statistics Research Conference. McConville has a background in establishment surveys and has previously worked as an American Statistical Association/National Science Foundation/Bureau of Labor Statistics research fellow. She has a B.A. degree in mathematics from Saint Olaf College and an M.A. and a Ph.D. in statistics from Colorado State University.

LEONARD I. NAKAMURA is emeritus economist of the Federal Reserve Bank of Philadelphia, after having served as vice-president and economist for more than 30 years. His research addresses financial economics and economic measurement issues, including intangibles, information flows, and free products. Previously, Nakamura led the research team responsible for producing the Business Outlook Survey, a regional manufacturing survey, and the State Coincident Indexes, as well as other economic indicators.

He also served as economist at Citibank and as senior economic consultant for The Conference Board. He has taught courses at the Wharton School of the University of Pennsylvania, Swarthmore College, and Bryn Mawr College, and was previously a faculty member at Rutgers University. He has a B.A. degree in social sciences from Swarthmore College and an M.A. and a Ph.D. in economics from Princeton University.

WESLEY YUNG is director of the Economic Statistics Methods Division of Statistics Canada. In this role, he manages a division of 110 methodologists who provide support to the Economic Statistics Field of Statistics Canada. Prior to this, he was assistant director of the division, where he managed 40 methodologists who provided support to annual and sub-annual business surveys and to the Tax Data Division. Yung also served as section chief and senior methodologist at Statistics Canada. While currently in a management position, he continues to remain active in survey methods research touching on variance estimation and, more recently, collection research. He has B.Sc. and M.Sc. degrees in statistics from Dalhousie University in Nova Scotia and a Ph.D. in statistics from Carleton University in Ontario.

COMMITTEE ON NATIONAL STATISTICS

The Committee on National Statistics was established in 1972 at the National Academies of Sciences, Engineering, and Medicine to improve the statistical methods and information on which public policy decisions are based. The committee carries out studies, workshops, and other activities to foster better measures and fuller understanding of the economy, the environment, public health, crime, education, immigration, poverty, welfare, and other public policy issues. It also evaluates ongoing statistical programs and tracks the statistical policy and coordinating activities of the federal government, serving a unique role at the intersection of statistics and public policy. The committee's work is supported by a consortium of federal agencies through a National Science Foundation grant, a National Agricultural Statistics Service cooperative agreement, and several individual contracts.